UFOs

Karin S. Coddon, *Book Editor*

Bruce Glassman, *Vice President*
Bonnie Szumski, *Publisher*
Helen Cothran, *Managing Editor*

GREENHAVEN PRESS
An imprint of Thomson Gale, a part of The Thomson Corporation

THOMSON
——✳——™
GALE

Detroit • New York • San Francisco • San Diego • New Haven, Conn.
Waterville, Maine • London • Munich

THOMSON
GALE

LIBRARY OF CONGRESS CATALOGING-IN-PUBLICATION DATA

UFOs / Karin S. Coddon, book editor.
   p. cm. — (At issue)
   Includes bibliographical references and index.
   ISBN 0-7377-2434-X (lib. : alk. paper) — ISBN 0-7377-2435-8 (pbk. : alk. paper)
   1. Unidentified flying objects. I. Coddon, Karin S. (Karin Susan) II. At issue (San Diego, Calif.)
   TL789.U218 2005
   001.942—dc22   2004052398

Printed in the United States of America

Contents

Introduction

On four consecutive December nights in 1980, U.S. Air Force personnel stationed at the Bentwaters base in Suffolk, England, investigated an unidentified craft that had hovered above and briefly landed in nearby Rendlesham Forest. Members of the base's security patrol reported strange darting lights, intermittent disruption of radio communications, and unusually high levels of radiation. One witness, Staff Sergeant James Penniston, got close enough to touch the bizarre craft that had landed in the woods. In notes he made at the time, Penniston described the object's glossy black surface and cryptic, hieroglyphic-like markings. When the craft suddenly, silently ascended, it left broken tree branches and conspicuous, tripodlike indentations in the forest earth. The air force officers filed reports describing the incidents of December 26–29, but both the U.S. and British military authorities concluded that the events in the forest were of no defense significance. Eyewitness Lieutenant Colonel Charles Halt's detailed memo on the incident, based on a tape recording he had made as he inspected the site, was suppressed by the U.S. government until a suit filed under the Freedom of Information Act led to its release to the general public in December 2002. The sightings in Rendlesham Forest have come to be known as "England's Roswell," referring to what is perhaps the most famous alleged UFO incident, the 1947 crash of a mysterious craft outside of Roswell, New Mexico.

One event, different interpretations

UFO skeptics—a group largely composed of scientists, government officials, and self-described "rationalists"—argue that UFO sightings such as those in Rendlesham have terrestrial explanations. They point to the lack of physical evidence and/or the dubious credibility of most eyewitnesses that typically characterize reported sightings. Extraterrestrial skeptics also argue that the military's secret development and testing of ultrasophisticated weaponry may also explain the appearance of "otherworldly" aircraft, often citing the Stealth bomber as an example. The official explanation of Rendlesham concludes that a rare convergence of high winds, atmospheric anomalies, and satellite debris combined with a lighthouse beacon several miles from the forest to create the appearance of an extraterrestrial phenomenon.

Yet many remain convinced that an extraterrestrial craft landed in Rendlesham. They insist that the usual arguments posed by skeptics cannot account for the incident. The Rendlesham craft had in fact left physical evidence in the form of broken tree limbs, impressions in the forest floor, and unusually high radiation readings in the area of the sighting. According to science writer Jim Wilson, "What the skeptics couldn't explain . . . is a scientific report found in the MOD [Ministry of Defense] files. It revealed radiation levels 25 times higher than normal background levels in the soil and trees surrounding the landing site." In addition, the primary witnesses were reliable. As members of the U.S. Air Force, they were neither inclined to embrace the notion of extraterrestrial visitation nor to misrecognize even the most technologically advanced, top-secret craft.

The continuing debate over UFOs

The passionate dispute over Rendlesham exemplifies the enduring controversy over the origins of unidentified flying objects. If the majority of both Americans and Canadians, for example, think that UFOs are extraterrestrial, mainstream science and journalism regard such an assumption as the stuff of fantasy fiction and pop culture mythology, an irrational if mostly harmless belief. Each side in the ongoing debate makes a strong case for its position, just as each side may be justifiably faulted for excesses that occasionally undermine the persuasiveness of its argument.

Those who support an extraterrestrial interpretation of UFOs cite the thousands of reported sightings. They also point to what they argue is a suspiciously high level of government secrecy concerning the matter starting with Project Blue Book, the joint military and intelligence program founded in 1947 to investigate the phenomena. Many believers claim that the U.S. government has deliberately concealed proof of extraterrestrial visitation because it has sought to utilize UFO supertechnology in the service of maintaining global military superiority. Some proponents of the extraterrestrial interpretation argue as well that such government deception is motivated by a desire to ward off the worldwide political, economic, and psychological chaos that might ensue from proof of intelligent life elsewhere in the universe. Much of the human race, accustomed to regarding itself as the pinnacle of a divine creation, could not cope with evidence of a superior species beyond earth.

Yet even many believers concede that the vast majority of UFO sightings may be easily attributed to naturally occurring or technologically feasible phenomena, including meteorites, atypical weather conditions, satellites, and experimental military aircraft. Numerous reported sightings have later been exposed as deliberate hoaxes or products of eyewitnesses' overactive imaginations. Skeptics frequently characterize believers as possessed by a cultlike zeal. As evidence they cite the Heaven's Gate mass suicides of 1997, in which a sect of UFO enthusiasts near San Diego, California, killed themselves in order to join what they were convinced was an alien spacecraft following the Hale-Bopp comet.

The alien abduction phenomenon

Accounts of alien abduction have further fueled the UFO controversy. In abduction accounts, individuals, usually placed under regression hypnosis designed to recover repressed memories, have related strikingly similar experiences of being taken away to a spaceship or eerie laboratory by extraterrestrials. There, invasive, quasimedical tests are performed on the human subject before he or she is eventually released unharmed and unremembering. Often, the goal of such experiments is believed to be hybridization of human and alien cells. Among the most prominent believers in alien abduction is Harvard psychiatrist John E. Mack. Mack states, "The alien abduction phenomenon is one among a number of manifestations . . . that are forcing us to appreciate that cosmic realities exist beyond the three-dimensional universe that has bounded our earthly existence."

However, critics question the validity of the regression hypnosis method employed in calling forth ostensible abduction memories. They point out that the same techniques gave rise to a wave of satanic ritual child abuse claims in the 1980s and 1990s, virtually all of which were eventually proven to be baseless. The "abductees" themselves, assert many critics, may genuinely believe in the reality of the experience recounted under hypnosis, and may suffer real distress that mimics the symptoms of posttraumatic stress disorder. Nonetheless, claims of alien abduction rely almost entirely on firsthand accounts rather than any physical evidence and are therefore questionable.

UFOs and the Cold War era

Both believers and skeptics believe the Cold War played a role in the UFO phenomenon. To many partisans on both sides, it seems no coincidence that the first two "modern" UFO sightings—by rescue pilot Kenneth Arnold over Washington's Cascade mountains and in the high desert outside of Roswell—occurred in 1947, the same year that the CIA was established with the express purpose of gathering intelligence against the Soviet Union and the newly formed People's Republic of China. Nonbelievers in the extraterrestrial interpretation argue that the U.S.-Soviet arms race spawned the development and secret deployment of numerous high-tech aircraft that could easily have been mistaken by an unsuspecting populace for "flying saucers" or other strange airborne objects. Many cultural scholars argue that the simultaneous proliferation both of reported UFO sightings and "alien invasion" movies such as *The War of the Worlds*, *Invaders from Mars*, and *Earth vs. the Flying Saucers* reflects the widespread Cold War–era anxiety about a sudden Russian invasion or nuclear attack.

Ufologists respond that descriptions of apparent extraterrestrial craft and beings may be found throughout recorded human history. They do not dispute, though, the significance of the Cold War. The crash of an alien spacecraft at Roswell, it is claimed, allowed the U.S. to recover from the wreckage superadvanced technology that the military secretly incorporated into its Cold War arsenal. Area 51, a top-secret airbase in the Nevada desert near Groom Lake, has long been rumored to be the site where the U.S. military tests crafts and weaponry employing alien technology obtained as a result of the Roswell crash.

"I want to believe" reads the caption on a poster of a flying saucer repeatedly shown on the 1990s television hit *The X-Files*, a show premised on the idea of a government conspiracy to conceal the fact of an alien invasion. The charge has been leveled against both extraterrestrial believers and skeptics that they are driven primarily by the *desire* to believe—either that UFOs come from alien worlds or that the modern scientific method is the ultimate arbiter of truth. Like the age-old debate between faith and reason, the dispute over the nature and origins of UFOs cannot—and perhaps should not—be easily resolved. In *At Issue: UFOs*, believers and skeptics make their best arguments for and against an extraterrestrial explanation for the UFO phenomenon.

1

UFO Sightings Are Hoaxes and Mistakes

Philip J. Klass, interviewed by Gary P. Posner

Philip J. Klass is a noted UFO investigator and skeptic. A former senior editor at Aviation Week & Space Technology, *Klass has written several books debunking UFO sightings and alien abduction claims, including* Ufos: The Public Deceived *and* The REAL Roswell Crashed Saucer Coverup. *Gary P. Posner is a physician and software company executive. He is the founder of the Tampa Bay Skeptics and has published extensively on claims of paranormal phenomena.*

In this interview, Philip J. Klass responds to critics who charge that his driving passion is to demonstrate that UFO reports are simple-minded hoaxes. Instead, he argues that the task of the skeptic is to conduct serious scientific investigation of claims rather than merely to act blindly on the desire to debunk UFOs. He also discounts accusations that he is part of a government conspiracy to hide the truth about the existence of UFOs. He states that in thirty-three years of investigating reports of UFOs, he has yet to find any credible evidence that extraterrestrials have visited Earth.

S̶keptic: One of the main raps against you is that, rather than acknowledging that a UFO case has no apparent prosaic explanation, you instead resort to crying "hoax."
    Klass: I never encountered a single hoaxer during my entire 10 years with GE [General Electric]. And in my first 14 years at *Av Week,* up until the time I began investigating UFO reports, I encountered only one spinner of tall tales. So, believe it or not,

Gary P. Posner, "ETs May Be *Out There* . . . but He Says They're *Not Here:* An Interview with Philip J. Klass, the World's Leading UFO Skeptic," *Skeptic,* vol. 7, 1999. Copyright © 1999 by Skeptic Magazine. Reproduced by permission.

when I first began looking at UFO reports, I naturally assumed that the witnesses were probably just honestly describing what they believed they had seen. But I quickly learned that I was too trusting.

Early investigations

My first major investigation was in 1966 when I visited Socorro, New Mexico. Two years earlier, a policeman—Lonnie Zamora—had reported witnessing an egg-shaped UFO land, two ETs in coveralls briefly scurry around, and then the UFO blast off like a rocket. Now at that time, I suspected that some glowing UFOs near high-tension power lines might be freak atmospheric phenomena which I called "plasma UFOs," similar to ball lightning. And I knew that the Socorro area frequently suffered intense thunderstorms. So, I suspected that Zamora might have seen a plasma. Dr. J. Allen Hynek had already briefly investigated this case for the Air Force's Project Blue Book [a U.S. Air Force investigation conducted from 1947 to 1969] and had rejected the possibility of a hoax, so that thought hadn't even entered my mind when I went down there.

But that began to change when an atmospheric physicist at the New Mexico Institute of Technology in Socorro told me that he hadn't even bothered to take the few minutes drive to the site. He explained to me how the town was economically depressed and that city officials were trying to attract industry, and urged me to "nose around" a bit. I soon learned that the local newspaper ran a box in every issue saying that the most efficient way to attract new industry is to first attract tourists. When I interviewed a man who lived right near the landing site, and had been working in his garden when the UFO supposedly blasted off, he told me that he hadn't heard a thing, and that when he visited the site soon afterwards he saw no physical evidence to support Zamora's story and suspected that it was a hoax. When I interviewed the police radio dispatcher who had taken Zamora's call for backup, he recalled that, strangely, Zamora had not requested a fellow police officer or someone from the Socorro sheriff's office, but instead asked that a specific state trooper be sent. And I found out that Socorro's mayor owned the "landing site" property and the town's only bank, and earlier had sought approval to build a new road to the UFO site for the benefit of tourists. So, when I wrote *UFOs: Identified*, I was confident enough to suggest that this case might be a hoax. And by the time my second UFO book, *UFOs Explained*, was published, I did unequivocally characterize the case as a hoax, as I've done subsequently regarding a number of other highly suspicious cases.

Skeptic: But the Socorro "tourist trap" was never built.

Klass: Yes, but the plan had been initiated. On the first anniversary of the "landing," a newspaper article quoted a city official as saying outright that they intended to use it as a tourist attraction, and it reported that the road to the site had recently been upgraded. It also mentioned that a movie about UFOs had recently shot some scenes in Socorro. Perhaps when members of the City Council learned the truth, they opted not to proceed any further with the plans.

> *When I first began looking at UFO reports, I naturally assumed that the witnesses were probably just honestly describing what they believed they had seen. But I quickly learned that I was too trusting.*

Skeptic: In *UFOs: Identified*, you actually endorsed a photo as a genuine "plasma UFO," only to later realize that *you* had been hoaxed. Might that embarrassment have caused you to become a bit too quick to cry "hoax"?

Klass: Too quick? I don't think so, no. But it sure taught me not to be too trusting of seemingly honest folks. That was the first UFO-photo case I ever investigated. A teenager named James Lucci had taken two nighttime photos of a glowing "plasma-looking" UFO in front of the moon. I saw them in John Fuller's *Incident At Exeter*, which was the first UFO book I ever read. But even though the pictures had been "authenticated" by a respected investigator with NICAP [National Investigations Committee on Aerial Phenomena], I felt I should make my own investigation. So I interviewed James and his older brother John, and afterwards I had no particular reason to doubt their word. I also spoke with their father, who was a professional photographer in the Air Force and had been in Europe when the photos were taken. He told me that he had no idea how anyone could fake photos like that. But one of them faintly resembled a kitchen saucer held in the palm of a hand.

So I asked James if he would allow me to photograph him in his front yard—where the UFO photos had been taken—with him holding a kitchen saucer. He flatly refused to do that, but he did agree to take a picture of *me* holding a saucer. But that photo, and some more like it that I took after I got home, were done in daylight, without a flash to make them "glow," and they didn't look anything like the Lucci photos. Then, shortly after my book was published, I learned that a photographic analyst for the University of Colorado's "Condon (UFO investigation) Committee" had managed to create a flash photo that looked somewhat similar to Lucci's. And sometime later, Robert Sheaffer created an even better one, and that finally convinced me that I had been "had." It wasn't until about 20 years later that John Lucci finally admitted to another investigator that the photos were indeed bogus.

Challenging cases

Skeptic: What case took the most time to find a solution?

Klass: I spent several years on the 1978 New Zealand case. That one received a lot of media coverage because of the videotape that was taken by a TV crew flying aboard a plane along the coastline. Dr. Bruce Maccabee, who's a well-known pro-UFO researcher and optics specialist, visited New Zealand and claimed that all of the diverse UFOs taped during that flight defied prosaic explanation. During the next few years, Bruce and I exchanged—and I'm not exaggerating—approximately 2,500 pages of single-spaced, typewritten letters about the details of this case. And while those exchanges were going on, I learned that after the incident, the pilot had had a suspicion that the longest-duration UFO—which resembled the full moon because it had been filmed with an out-of-focus telephoto lens—might have actually been one of the Japanese squid boats that use intense illumination to attract the squid. And when the pilot checked the official records, he found that one Japanese squid boat captain had registered his intention to fish in the vicinity of Christchurch, NZ, where the UFO was filmed. Part of the case had also involved "radar-blip" UFOs detected during an earlier flight. But a New Zealand scientist found that this particular radar often displayed spurious blips, some from surface ships and trains, under temperature-inversion atmospheric conditions. I even included a photo showing spurious blips on the same radar screen in my book, *UFOs: The Public Deceived,* which contains three entire chapters on this complex case. But in spite of all that, Maccabee rejected the Japanese squid-boat explanation, and declared the case inexplicable in prosaic terms. And not long after that, he endorsed the two dozen "hokey-looking" UFO photos taken by Ed Walters in Gulf Breeze, Florida, which many pro-UFOlogists now agree are double-exposure hoaxes. . . .

The government connection

Skeptic: You've been accused of being a "disinformation agent" of the government, or of the "military-industrial complex." So, the charges go, if you knew that our government really did possess a crashed saucer, you would work to keep the story buried so that other countries, and their industries, couldn't get their hands on that technology.

Klass: I do admit that a certain government agency pays me $100,000,000 per year *plus* taxi fare. But the money goes into a secret Swiss bank account whose number I've forgotten—and the agency refuses to provide it to me again. But, seriously, there's no way Washington could keep a story like that a secret for long, considering how many military and industry scientists would need to be involved. For example, back in the late '60s I learned that the Atomic Energy Commission [AEC] was worried that anti-Vietnam-war protesters might try to hijack a truck carrying nuclear weapons. The AEC even sought White House approval to deploy its own satellite system so it could continuously monitor the location of its trucks. I decided it best to "sit" on that story, but within several weeks it had leaked to the *Washington Post.* Look, if a UFO were to crash in the U.S., another might crash in the USSR, or Cuba, or China, or Switzerland, and one of those governments might opt to exploit the incident publicly rather than keeping it under wraps. So, while I might "sit" on a secret like that for a few days or a few weeks, I would then write the article for *Av Week* and graciously accept my Pulitzer Prize.

Skeptic: Some researchers claim that they *do* have military sources who confirm the existence of a crashed saucer. Hypothetically, of course, if official Washington were somehow managing to otherwise keep the facts secret, would you continue to "sit" on the story until the truth came out in the *Post*?

Klass: I consider this a bit hyper-hypothetical. But, if you insist, the answer is "not for long," for the reasons I just cited.

The only secrets that can be successfully kept secret are those known to *only one* person.

Skeptic: But, hyper-hypothetically, suppose you were to discover tomorrow that, in the name of national security, the government truly has been covering up the existence of a crashed saucer at Area 51 [top-secret military base in Nevada rumored to be the site of experiments with UFO technology]. Would you publish the story, or "sit" on it?

Klass: I'd first try to find out when it had been recovered: if within the past few days, I'd sit on it briefly and talk to sources to find out what the government planned to do. But if it had been recovered some weeks, or years, earlier, I'd also talk to sources, but then I'd rush to my PC to write the greatest story of my career.

Skeptic: So you'd break the story even if, hyper-hypothetically, the government had successfully kept this alien technology confined to Area 51 for the past 50 years?

Klass: Yes, indeed, and it would be, by far, the most exciting story of my life.

> *There's no way Washington could keep a story like that a secret for long, considering how many military and industry scientists would need to be involved.*

Skeptic: Considering your position with *Aviation Week & Space Technology* magazine, are you privy to what sort of top-secret activity really goes on at Area 51?

Klass: I've never been there, but I know it's where we first tested our then-secret U-2, and later our SR-71, spy planes, and more recently our F-117A stealth fighter. Undoubtedly it's used for flight tests of experimental aircraft of novel designs. And I believe it's also used for testing new types of decoy flares to protect our aircraft against enemy infrared-guided missiles. That whole area is a part of Nellis Air Force Base, where they periodically conduct simulated combat training exercises to evaluate our latest tactics and electronic countermeasures against simulated enemy anti-aircraft missiles. I think experimental planes might account for a few of the UFO reports generated from there, and the flare decoys probably account for others.

Skeptic: Have *you* ever seen anything in the sky that had you puzzled?

Klass: Yes, several times. The most recent was in 1995 near Seattle, where I was scheduled to give a UFO lecture to the local chapter of the Institute of Electrical and Electronics Engineers. It was about 7:25 p.m., shortly before my lecture, and I was standing outside chatting with several attendees when one of them pointed to the sky and asked, "What's that?" I saw what appeared to be an orangish, structured object that was just hovering there. Someone said, "It's a kite," but I responded, "No, it's at much too high an altitude," which I estimated to be at least several thousand feet. I thought it might be a weather balloon illuminated by the setting sun, but someone said, "No, it can't be. It's not moving." Then suddenly one of the men said, "I think I have binoculars in my car," and he went to retrieve them. A few moments later he returned and announced, "It's a kite," and handed me the binoculars. He was correct. But if not for those binoculars, I would have to "admit" that I had seen a UFO that I could not positively identify. But it wasn't doing anything extraordinary, like flying at hypersonic speed or making right-angle turns, so I would have assumed that this UFO had a prosaic explanation.

Disagreements among skeptics

Skeptic: Some of your critics harp about the absence of "internal criticism" among the "skeptics"—how we always agree with each other on everything. Have you ever found the work of a fellow skeptic worthy of criticism?

Klass: Jim Oberg, whom I greatly admire and have worked with—for example, in debunking the claim that Korean Air Lines 007 was on an espionage mission when it was shot down by the Soviets—has claimed that the U.S. government has used UFOs as "disinformation" to hide "black projects." I disagree with him on that, for the most part. If, before the existence of our "Stealth" program was made public, a person reported seeing a strange-looking, triangular-shaped craft, I wouldn't have expected the Air Force to issue a public statement to the effect that the object was not a "UFO" but an F-117A. So perhaps Oberg is correct about a few rare instances such as this. But I don't believe such disinformation has been widespread. And I have challenged Martin Kottmeyer on his theory that Kenneth Arnold's flying discs were probably a squadron of geese or other birds. But, to my knowledge, I have never encountered false-hoods or coverup of data when dealing with a fellow skeptic.

Skeptic: It was Kenneth Arnold's sighting in 1947 that inspired the term "flying saucers." You said that you disagree with a skeptic who thinks Arnold saw a formation of birds, but I've read where you suspect that he might have seen fragments of a glowing meteor breaking up in the atmosphere. Shouldn't a pilot be able to tell a glowing fireball from a non-glowing craft?

Klass: Surprisingly not. For example, in 1969 two airliner crews and a military fighter pilot flying near St. Louis did indeed mistake a glowing meteor-fireball, along with its several fragments, for a squadron of "UFOs." Fortunately, an alert newspaper photographer near Peoria managed to get a good photo of the meteor-fireball and one of its fragments. Otherwise, this incident could well have become a classic UFO case. The pilots all reported that the UFOs nearly collided with them, even though the photograph and other sighting reports showed that the meteor was at least 125 miles north of the aircraft.

> *In 1969 two airliner crews and a military fighter pilot flying near St. Louis did indeed mistake a glowing meteor-fireball, along with its several fragments, for a squadron of 'UFOs.'*

Skeptic: The famous case from July 1952, when UFOs were picked up on radar for several nights over Washington, DC, got a boost last year [1998] from the Fund for UFO Research. Has their report caused you to change your opinion of what really happened there?

Klass: Not at all. The report's Introduction contains elementary errors, such as confusing "temperature inversions" with "mirages." And the body of the report doesn't make the case. The confusing echoes picked up on the radar screens were most certainly the result of false propagation due to "temperature inversion." The following year the CAA [Civil Aviation Agency]—which is now the FAA [Federal Aviation Agency]—reported that just a month after the Washington incidents, its investigators monitored similar anomalous echoes on a radar scope in Washington during another hot, humid spell. Early radar was prone to this sort of problem, but since digital processors were introduced about 20 years ago, "radar UFO" cases have almost disappeared.

Skeptic: But during the DC case, didn't some pilots report seeing the "UFOs" as they were also being tracked on radar?

Klass: No. As a matter of fact, about 20 years ago I received a letter from one of the pilots who had been "scrambled" to Washington in his F-94 interceptor on one of those nights. He saw nothing in the sky, but said that the pilot of a companion F-94 did report seeing several lights. But that plane was flying at extremely low altitude and, the letter said, the other pilot had likely seen headlights from vehicles on the ground that were driving up enough of a slope to make their lights visible from the air.

The real Roswell coverup

Skeptic: In your book about the Roswell case,[1] you agree that there has been a coverup—not by the government—but by the pro-UFOlogists and the media! That sounds 180 degrees out of phase from the prevailing public opinion.

Klass: I certainly don't level the charge of "coverup" against all pro-UFOlogists on all cases. But I do accuse other Roswell book authors of coverup, as I do the TV shows that interviewed me for their "Roswell" reports and edited out, like those book authors, the key facts. Here's what I mean. They like to cite documents such as the formerly "Secret" September 1947 memo, to a top Air Force intelligence official at the Pentagon, from Lt. Gen. Nathan Twining, in which he expressed his view that UFOs are "something real" and not imaginary. But three major pro-Roswell books of which I am aware all managed to leave out the portion of Twining's note in which he laments "the lack of physical evidence" such as crashed-saucer fragments that would provide "undeniable proof" of the existence of UFOs. And this memo was written more than *two months after* the saucer supposedly had crashed at Roswell. Twining would certainly have known if such an event had really occurred—he was commander of the Air Materiel Command at Wright Field (now Wright-Patterson AFB) in Dayton, which was the center of the Air Force's top technical experts and laboratories and also where its Foreign Technology Intelligence

---

1. refers to findings of some strange debris in New Mexico in 1947 that many believe was a crashed alien spacecraft

Center was located. And there are other formerly classified government documents from the late 1940s—after the '47 Roswell incident—that convey similar frustration of top officials about the absence of any physical evidence which would prove beyond a doubt that some UFO reports involved craft and help identify their origin. When CBS's *48 Hours* [news show] taped me for a segment on Roswell that aired in 1994, I even held up one of those "Top Secret" documents to the camera, pointing out the relevant passages. But, for obvious reasons, they edited out that entire portion of the interview. . . .

Problems with "abduction" accounts

Skeptic: Ironically, some of your best "sources" are members of the pro-UFO community. Why do you think they confide in the "devil incarnate"?

Klass: Many of them have become sorely distressed over the growing credulity of the UFO Movement's current leadership. For example, the strong endorsement by MUFON's [Mutual UFO Network] leaders and Bruce Maccabee of the Gulf Breeze photos, and the current focus on UFO "abduction" tales and crashed-saucer coverups. When I attend a MUFON conference, invariably several people will approach me to say things like, "Keep up the good work" and "Thanks for keeping us honest."

Skeptic: In your book *UFO Abductions: A Dangerous Game*, you say that no one need fear being abducted by ETs unless they want to be abducted, because the experience is just a fantasy. Have you ever had occasion to look a troubled "abductee" in the eye—perhaps a patient of Dr. John Mack or one of the other abduction specialists—and say that?

Klass: Having spent more than 33 years investigating some of the most impressive UFO reports, without ever finding any credible evidence of ET visits, certainly that influences my views on people who claim to have been abducted by ETs. I've done several TV talk shows with "abductees," but the hectic pace of the shows never offered the opportunity for on-camera confrontation, and they never linger on after the show to talk with me. However, shortly after publication of my book, I received a phone call from a young woman who had been involved in an "abductee support group" in the Washington area. Her father had given her a copy of the book to read, and she called to thank me for "opening her eyes to reality." Not too long after that, I received a letter from a Boston man who had

had a similar experience and thanked me for writing the book. But, on the other hand, several years ago I received a phone call from a psychotherapist in North Carolina whose patient—a 30ish divorcee with an 8-year-old son—had been referred to him by her medical doctor who had found a small growth that needed to be removed from the base of her brain. But the woman believed that it was an "alien implant" that should stay there until the ETs wanted to remove it themselves. Her doctor had suggested the psychotherapist, who had bought my book, and who gave it to the patient to read. So he called me to ask if I was willing to talk with her. He mentioned that her young son was now afraid to go out at night, fearing he too might be abducted. Anyway, several weeks later the woman called. I had hoped that, while she might still be inclined to believe, my book would have opened her eyes to a prosaic option. But instead, she bitterly attacked me for questioning that she had been selected for abduction by the ETs. And after about 15 minutes of that, I signed off, and I've never heard further from her or her psychotherapist. I wrote to him a couple years ago seeking an update, but never heard back. So, you win some, you lose some.

Skeptic: Can anyone ever really *prove* that UFOs—and the aliens, and the abductions, and the implants, and the painful needle extraction of eggs and sperm in order to breed alien-human hybrids—aren't real?

Klass: When I first entered the UFO field in the mid-'60s, there were lots of interesting "nuts and bolts" type cases involving civilian and military pilots, radar, etc., where I could apply my avionics training and expertise. In those days there were relatively few hoaxes and many more instances of misidentification. If someone were to report to NICAP that they had seen a UFO flying over the White House at noon, NICAP would question that claim because of the lack of other witnesses. NICAP's director, Maj. Donald Keyhoe, questioned the Betty and Barney Hill abduction claim,[2] and NICAP officials were reluctant to fully endorse the Socorro case because of Zamora's report of seeing two creatures. And in those days, if a person reported several UFO sightings, NICAP would characterize them as a "repeater," and treat their claim with extra caution. But today the situation is vastly different. People like

2. Betty and Barney Hill were a New England couple who reported sighting a UFO in 1964 and, through hypnosis, had memories of being abducted by aliens.

Budd Hopkins are putting the focus on UFO "abductions" and the claim that ETs can make themselves and their "abductees" invisible and can transport their victims through brick walls and glass windows. One of Dr. John Mack's "abductees" claims that she has been taken aboard a UFO *more than 100 times*, and even that doesn't prompt Mack to question her tales.

UFOs are not real

Skeptic: And what would you say to those critics who claim that you are motivated by some sort of "hatred" or "fear" of the idea that UFOs and ET visitations might be real?

Klass: As I turn 80, my fondest hope is that a genuine ET craft will land on our back patio and that I will be abducted. Hopefully, with the ETs' advanced technology and knowledge, they will be able to cure my spinal and walking problems and the damage to my vocal cord. Of course, I would have to pay [nuclear physicist and leading ufologist] Stanton Friedman $10,000—based on my long-standing wager that UFOs will never be proven real—but I would expect to become wealthy from the royalties of a new book titled *Why Me, ET?* And instead of spending many hours each week "debunking" UFOs, I'll finally have time to watch some TV, go to the movies, and perhaps get to read a few non-UFO books for enjoyment. I even keep my videocam near my bed in the hopes of being able to film a beautiful "Nordic-type" ET extracting sperm "the old-fashioned way."

2

Government Agencies Hide the Truth About Ufos

Jim Marrs

Dallas journalist and author Jim Marrs has written exten-sively on UFOs and government conspiracies. His books in-clude Alien Agenda: Investigating the Extraterrestrial Presence Among Us.

At the dawn of the twenty-first century, evidence of ex-traterrestrial visitations abounds, despite the concerted efforts of skeptics to discount it. Although officially denying the extraterrestrial origins of UFOs, America's military, government, and scientific elites have been se-cretly investigating the phenomena since 1947, when a mysterious craft crashed in Roswell, New Mexico. At the same time, the government may be trying to con-dition the public to the idea that there are aliens on the planet by encouraging stories about them in the popu-lar media. Humanity's search for life elsewhere in the cosmos has a spiritual dimension. People are seeking a transcendant understanding of the universe that goes beyond intellectual knowledge.

A s the twentieth century draws to a close, cattle mutilations continue, crop circles are more elaborate than in the past, and the abduction experience appears to be more widespread than ever, in spite of the debunkers and media-supported pub-lic disbelief.

The UFO issue appears to be coming to a head. New realities

Jim Marrs, *Alien Agenda: Investigating the Extraterrestrial Presence Among Us.* New York: HarperPaperbacks, 1997. Copyright © 1997 by Jim Marrs. All rights reserved. Reproduced by permission of HarperCollins Publishers, Inc.

are impinging upon our collective consciousness.
increasingly accepted by all but the most intra
are that there is much more to life than our own bᵣᵢₓ
existence on Earth and that we are not alone on our worₗₓ.

A wealth of evidence

The concept that we are not alone is supported by overwhelm-
ing evidence, including multitudinous sightings, photographs,
films and video, radar contacts, personal confrontations, abduction reports, crop circles, animal mutilations, channeled
messages, multiple-witness reports, and physical evidence such
as indented landing sites, holes in the ground, burned vegeta-
tion, human scars, and implants. Some of the human reports
and photographic evidence undoubtedly are the product of
misinterpretation or hoaxers, but the sheer number and consistency of descriptions argues against all of them being mis-
takes or fakes.

> *// Although there is no clear indication that such
> technology was the product of alien visitation
> rather than some lost civilization of man, the
> many ancient tales of sky-gods and their flying
> craft tip the scales in favor of alien contact. //*

Another argument supporting the idea of nonhuman visitors is the longevity of the reports. If sightings had occurred
only in recent times, they might be attributable to some passing mass psychosis, an aberrant copycat function of minds
frightened by the onrush of modern technology. But reports of
flying machines and unearthly visitors predate man's history.
And the evidence of technology superior to ours in the distant
past is particularly compelling. Although there is no clear indi-
cation that such technology was the product of alien visitation
rather than some lost civilization of man, the many ancient
tales of sky-gods and their flying craft tip the scales in favor of
alien contact.

The possibility of ancient astronauts provides not only a
credible explanation for legends and strange artifacts in man's
history but also for the documented anomalies on the moon

and Mars—some of which appear strikingly similar to our own mysterious Great Pyramid.

It would seem that early UFOs were viewed and reported through the perspective of the times in which they were observed. Thus, it was only near mid-twentieth century that UFOs began to take the form of flying machines. In view of the sum total of evidence available today, it would appear that the earth is being visited by a wide variety of craft bearing many different species. This created confusion in the past because most people had trouble conceiving of even one type of visitor to Earth.

There can be no doubt that beginning at least with World War II, military and government authorities in the United States took a keen interest in reports of flying craft and the glowing orbs that chased warplanes. Much material exists to suggest that the leaders of Nazi Germany may have developed a flying saucer based on advanced technology, which ended up in the hands of another nation. Whether this saucer was the result of human ingenuity or perhaps alien contact has yet to be determined.

The year 1947 marked an obvious turning point in the government's attitude toward the subject, adding considerable weight to speculation that something unearthly was recovered near Roswell, New Mexico, and perhaps other locations. Where the government had acknowledged the possibility of extraterrestrial craft and beings prior to 1947, a new attitude of dismissal and ridicule was instituted. Right up to today, official denial has effectively blocked any public consideration of the phenomenon. Yet consistent internal reports and testimony from a variety of people showed that official interest in UFOs at the highest levels of government never diminished—only went deep undercover.

A policy of denial

The Brookings report [an official report denying UFOs] coupled with numerous public statements by several different officials indicated that leaders were fearful of the knowledge they had concerning UFOs. They feared disruption of public institutions and panic. Military officers, as always, viewed exotic technology as potential weapon systems to be kept secret from any potential enemy. Other leaders may have been less concerned about the public's state of mind or military security than about their own interests in maintaining control over public institutions, technologies, and profits.

It is clear from the record that beginning in 1952, government intelligence, initially the CIA, began to assume control over the UFO issue. U.S. Air Force Project Blue Book [US Air Force investigation of UFOs spanning from 1947 to 1969] became merely a public relations front with a twofold purpose: to quiet the public clamor by dismissing as many UFO reports as possible and yet at the same time quietly collecting serious UFO information that was passed along to higher authorities.

> *Strange alien creatures have been showing up in everything from expensive Super Bowl TV ads and children's cartoons to series such as* The X-Files *and* Dark Skies, *not to mention blockbuster movies.*

It appears highly plausible that about this same time, a top-level, highly secret group of military officers, scientists, and other leaders was established to study the UFO issue—an MJ-12 group [top-secret "Operation Majestic-12," a Truman-era project investigating UFOs] in effect if not in name. According to a wide variety of sources, such a group still operates today. Such a group would more clearly represent the wealthy top 2 percent of the United States population than the bottom 98 percent, and it is fair to assume that their interests—particularly from the standpoint of self-survival—might not coincide with the best interests of the general public. Then there are the bizarre stories—from too many different sources to ignore—that at some point representatives of the government may have in fact made contact with aliens.

Aliens in pop culture

All of this would presuppose the tightest secrecy possible by government—exactly the situation discerned by a study of the historical record. However, this wall of silence may have developed some cracks in recent years. It may be that our leaders are making sporadic efforts to condition the public to the idea of alien visitation. Strange alien creatures have been showing up in everything from expensive Super Bowl TV ads and children's cartoons to series such as *The X-Files* and *Dark Skies*, not to mention blockbuster movies. While the profit motive undoubtedly plays a large part, that such airings are allowed indicates to many that such concepts are being encouraged by the leadership of the tightly controlled mass media.

> *❝The alien agenda obviously encompasses much more than one race seeking to enslave or exploit the earth.❞*

A truly free and democratic people—such as we like to think of ourselves being—should assert their right to the same knowledge as the wealthiest members of society. After all, we will all share equally in the future of Earth. It could very well be that the reason so many ordinary people claim to have had contact with alien beings is that those human leaders who have sought to keep the public ignorant of the alien presence are being bypassed.

Despite what appears to be a concerted effort by government and others to hide away this alien presence, an ever-growing number of people are becoming conscious of this new reality through a variety of means, including personal contact, channeled messages, the wider dissemination of news and information through computer networks, books, movies, TV, videos, a growing number of public speakers, plain old intuition, and military-developed remote viewing.

A spiritual reality

A consistent message is becoming clear—we are all free-willed multidimensional beings composed of both the physical and the spiritual. Our individual bodies are made up of physical matter that must conform to physical laws. But our bodies are energized by a thinking form of energy—the soul, if you prefer—which, like all energy, can neither be created nor destroyed, only change form. Many researchers into our spiritual side believe that mankind is in the process of shifting into a higher plane of existence—one that deals from the heart, not the intellect.

Our multidimensional side has blocked conscious memory of our true nature because of the lessons to be learned during our physical existence on Earth. At the level of this sentient and creative energy, we are all—humans as well as all other life-forms in the universe—connected in some type of comprehensive energy grid, akin to Einstein's unified field theory. This appears to operate at the submolecular level or beyond, which our science is only just now discovering. It is at this level that man's intuitive and psychic abilities come into play. According to nearly all personal reports, most alien beings are more aware of this reality than ourselves, which may explain their apparent delicate handling of the contact between us.

> **❝** *Many feel that the aliens of energy and light, called the Transcendentals by the remote viewers, are here to witness—and perhaps help—our shift to new realities.* **❞**

This could also explain why there has been no direct *Independence Day*–type attack [1996 science fiction movie] or physical attempt to subjugate humanity. After all, if their intentions were hostile, common sense dictates that they would have moved against us much earlier than today when they would face our deep space platforms and "Star Wars" weaponry.

This may also explain misconceptions regarding the abductions. Many believers in this all-are-one concept contend that abductees have agreed to work with the alien greys at one of the basic unconscious levels. Yet, when contact is made, the conscious mind is terrified at the experience. "Besides," commented one metaphysical student, "the greys have no bedside manner." The greys are trying to learn to deal with humans. They are probably puzzled that abductees feel abused by their medical experiments. Additionally, according to some researchers, the greys are living in a state of fear, and that fear is often reflected by the humans they contact.

New levels of consciousness are needed

It has been said that they must learn to reach higher levels of consciousness through the heart, not through the mind. It is ironic that apparently the only way they know how to learn about love and emotion is through cold, intellectual study. It's a bit like trying to teach someone to dance—you can explain about steps and count all you want but unless they have rhythm, forget it.

The alien agenda obviously encompasses much more than one race seeking to enslave or exploit the earth. Considering all accounts, there are many different races visiting us today, apparently for many different reasons—some benign and helpful, others perhaps more selfish. No one motive can be established any more than a Fiji Islander could ascribe one motive to the many travelers daily flying high over his head on trans-Pacific jetliners.

Whatever the motivations and whatever the technology in use, this agenda involves all concerned, human and otherwise, and it involves the prime creative force in the universe—the creator of all. As abductee Judy Doraty was told by an alien grey when she asked about God, "He's the same to us as He is to you."

It would appear that religion—or more specifically spiritualism—is interconnected with the alien agenda. While most religions address facets of spiritual truth, none can claim exclusive knowledge. The world's religions can be compared to the story of the blind men and the elephant. They all have a piece of the truth, but their interpretations may not be on the mark. Today, many feel that organized religion is about the control of understanding. It is the mind of man trying to interpret the heart of God—and not doing a very good job of it.

The constraints of fear

It has been said that every human feeling originates from only two basic emotions—love or fear. Love, the basis of compassion, sympathy, and understanding, stems from man's highest energy level, while fear, the producer of intolerance, hatred, and violence, comes from our basest energy level. Love, said to flow from God, is of the heart. Fear is a product of the mind. Unfortunately, too many religions focus on fear—fear of Satan, fear of death, and fear of the afterlife—to control members.

All of humanity may be moving into a higher consciousness. Some call it "Christ-Consciousness." There is no question that the old order—the old systems, the old ways of doing things—is crumbling. New dimensions, new realities are on the horizon. And each of us has a role to play. Mankind is only as strong as its weakest link. There are no victims or castaways.

Everyone is involved. Each of us is like a tuning fork. When one resonates with the higher frequency of heartfelt love and understanding, others follow.

Many feel that the aliens of energy and light, called the Transcendentals by the remote viewers, are here to witness—and perhaps help—our shift to new realities. It is literally a rebirth and, like any birth, there will be pain as we all move through the physical transitions. Fear will only make it worse. Yet, fear will continue to be a large part of our experience until we are able to break through the government secrecy and media-driven illusion of life to gain full knowledge of our world, our true history, our future, and our relationship with others in the universe.

A wake-up call to humanity

The advent of the UFO phenomenon on our collective consciousness in recent years may well be a wake-up call—a not-so-subtle message that human intellectual knowledge is not the end-all of existence or any assurance of peace and tranquillity. It won't be proven with a slide rule nor seen in a telescope. For true love and understanding, the basis for everything good and desirable, we must look inward. We all know truth when we hear it. It resonates deep within the individual being. We will know it by the subtle signals from the heart.

Mankind in its present growth phase might be compared to the college student, who as a freshman believes she knows everything but as a senior realizes she knows very little. Our adolescence is coming to an end and it is time to break free from Mommy and Daddy—all dogmatic authority figures—and begin to take our rightful place as freethinking and responsible members of a universal public.

After all, to anyone not from Earth, we are the aliens—and fearsome ones at that with our primitive and destructive ways. Perhaps we are the focus of universal concern and are all being guided by a host of nonhuman life-forms.

To paraphrase that great possum philosopher Pogo, "We have found the alien agenda and it is about us."

3

The U.S. Government Has Not Tried to Hide Evidence of Extraterrestrials

Roy Craig

Roy Craig holds a PhD in physical chemistry from Iowa State University. A World War II veteran, he has worked as a university professor, weapons expert, and technical and environmental consultant. Craig was a key participant in the Condon Study, a scientific investigation of UFO phenomena sponsored by the U.S. Air Force and University of Colorado.

Many people who believe in UFOs also think that the U.S. government is engaged in a conspiracy to conceal irrefutable proof of extraterrestrials. Since 1947 the military and the CIA have been involved in secret research and development programs, some of them focused on determining the origins of UFOs. It is impossible that an operation to cover up extraterrestrial evidence involving thousands of government agents could have remained unbreached for fifty years. In reality, the U.S military was being secretive because it was investigating the Soviet Union's satellite program during the time of the Cold War.

I found different individuals and groups of individuals referring to each other as "kooks" and regretting the fact that kooks were associated with their serious interests in flying saucers. One civilian organization even notified us that it had its

Roy Craig, *UFOs: An Insider's View of the Official Quest for Evidence.* Denton: University of North Texas Press, 1995. Copyright © 1995 by Roy Craig. All rights reserved. Reproduced by permission.

own undercover agent checking into some of the "kook" groups.

It was obvious, of course, that some of the people with whom I visited required little or no evidence as a basis for belief, and that others were taking advantage of that situation. Stories of trips on flying saucers, physical contact with "men" from outer space, and telepathic contact with outer space intelligences were related to me at various times. Often the people relating these experiences apparently were convinced, in their own minds, that the experiences were real and their accounts true. Internal incompatibilities or contradictions in the accounts were accepted without concern.

Perhaps these people have psychiatric problems. Yet we all have our hang-ups, on one subject or another. Are the miraculous tales related by these people fundamentally different in nature from those which millions of Americans find admirable on Sunday mornings?

Grounds for suspicion

A large organization of UFO believers which traditionally subscribed to the Air Force conspiracy theory included, in its leadership and advisers, retired military officers, acting business executives, scientists, engineers, and others whose judgment is generally considered sound and reliable. Some had held such positions as Air Force Public Information Officer or executive officer of the Central Intelligence Agency (CIA) itself, and had been concerned with UFOs in one way or another while in those positions. One would not expect such men to accuse the Air Force of hiding the truth without grounds for the belief. Are their grounds valid? Is this a problem of paranoia or is it justifiable concern?

In January, 1953, the CIA had convened a panel of scientists to review UFO information and files and render judgment regarding the nature of the UFO problem.

The U.S. Government did succeed in keeping the development of atomic bombs secret even from the people who were doing the work of purifying the enriched uranium and plutonium of which the bombs were composed. I remember conversations in 1952 with women at Oak Ridge, Tennessee, who worked on the chemical processing of weapon-grade uranium-235. In the early days of this work, they were making the ingredients of the first atomic bomb. All they knew, however, is that they were working with "T," and one drop of the solution they processed was worth the price of a Cadillac. Government agencies do keep secrets from the government's people, mostly under the guise of national security requirements. With examples of secrecy readily at hand, is it irrational to conclude that agencies of our government might attempt to hide the truth about UFOs from the public?

The role of the CIA

Historically, the CIA was known to have been involved with the UFO question. In January, 1953, the CIA had convened a panel of scientists to review UFO information and files and render judgment regarding the nature of the UFO problem A censored version of the report had been declassified. Although the CIA was involved in 1953, it was not obvious that it had retained a specific interest in UFOs through the 1960s. If it had, and, as the other large organization of UFO believers maintained, if it had conspired to deceive the public about UFOs, the Colorado project [1967 University of Colorado study of UFO incidents] would necessarily have been a tool of the conspiracy. When the founders of this UFO organization revealed, at an evening social gathering, that they not only held that position but also believed the CIA representative on the project was to be none other than the project director himself, that suggestion struck me as being comically absurd. Unfortunately, it was absurd, and patently so, only because I knew the character of the director, and not on other grounds. The CIA, established by the National Security Act of 1947 with the stipulation that it would have no internal security functions, was, by 1951, secretly recruiting scientists to "take any job you want, with any university, corporation, or department—just report to us and collect a decent income." Their recruiter said those words to me, in sworn secrecy, when I was about to receive a graduate degree from Iowa State University. The thought that some member of our project could be reporting secretly to the CIA was, therefore, in itself not irrational.

As I pondered the various conspiracy theories, thoughts of

secret activities I knew of in this nation, including the work of thousands of agents whom American citizens are paying to build up personal information dossiers on American citizens, entered the consideration. These thoughts combined with others regarding covert military expenditures and activities. I could not help but wonder if a good psychoanalyst would have to judge the society itself as paranoid.

No proof of a conspiracy

While I could not dismiss the conspiracy theories on the basis of individual or group paranoia, a little thought convinced me that the fact of extraterrestrial visitation, if it were a fact, could not successfully be concealed for long by either the Air Force or the CIA. That conviction was strengthened by the Echo Flight Incident experience[1] of having quite secret information pound upon my own unauthorized ears when a UFO was rumored to be involved in the secret event. I do not believe that human beings with knowledge of an event of such fantastic significance as extraterrestrial visitation would be capable of refraining from revealing that information for long. Dr. Condon [Edward Uhler, head of the Colorado Project investigating UFOs] had said, when we pointedly asked him if he would reveal the fact to the public if we came up with firm evidence of real extraterrestrial presence: "Well, I guess I'd phone the Secretary of the Air Force and say, 'We got it—what are you folks going to do with it?'" Dr. Condon was once quoted by the press as saying that the discovery of an extraterrestrial being would be perhaps the greatest discovery of all time—one that he would be perfectly happy to make. While he would have been willing to allow the Air Force or others to reveal this discovery to the public in a manner which avoided panic and chaos, would he have been willing to have the information kept hidden for all time, and not receive public acknowledgment of his discovery? Not likely.

Dr. Condon also had given consideration to UFO conspiracy theories. In a letter to Dr. Walter Orr Roberts, then Board Chairman of the American Association for the Advancement of Science, written after completion of the Colorado study, he wrote:

> These people [UFO buffs] in varying degrees insist
> that visitors are coming to Earth in flying saucers

1. UFO sightings in 1967 at a Montana air force base that precipitated a mysterious shutdown of all Echo flight missiles

from other civilizations. Some insist that this is known to our government and that the truth is being deliberately held back from the public. After careful study I conclude that there is no scientifically valid evidence in support of either proposition. Notice that I do not say that no such evidence will ever be found; simply that none is available now.

In search of little green men

One of the most intriguing stories involved in the Air Force conspiracy belief is the tale of the little green men who were taken from the site of a flying saucer crash near Aztec, New Mexico. The aliens' frozen bodies supposedly are kept in Hangar 19, or some other specific location, at Wright-Patterson Air Base. (A similar story is told about a Roswell, New Mexico, site.)

> *One of the most intriguing stories involved in the Air Force conspiracy belief is the tale of the little green men who were taken from the site of a flying saucer crash near Aztec, New Mexico.*

While working on the Colorado UFO Project, I visited Wright-Patterson to review the files of Project Blue Book [an earlier Air Force UFO Investigation]. I was not so naive as to think that if a tank full of frozen green men were kept secretly in Hangar 19, I would be able to learn that fact by direct questions to the keepers of the secret, or by sneaking a peek into whatever hanger or building in which they were supposedly kept. I was constantly watching, however, for small slips of the tongue or references to information we were not supposed to know about.

What I found at Project Blue Book was little concern by Major Quintanilla, who was in charge of the project at that time, or by anyone else there, about the fact that public reports of UFO sightings were not investigated seriously by a great number of the "UFO Officers," one officer being so designated at each air base. Their interest was intense, however, in details of any report which might have been triggered by a satellite in decaying orbit and burning as it reentered the atmosphere. Blue Book personnel actively searched for pieces of reentered satellite, for the obvious and practical reason of learning what materials of construction the Russians were then using in their satellite program.

Persistent believers

As for the little green men, I next became involved in the tale ten years after completion of the Colorado study. We had purchased and moved onto the historic La Boca Ranch, on the western Colorado-New Mexico border. A gentleman who subscribed to the Air Force conspiracy belief appeared at my door, wanting to talk about UFOs. As we talked, and as he looked around the ranch headquarters and the site where the railroad station had been, I became aware that he was surreptitiously seeking confirmation of his belief that the saucer which crashed near Aztec, along with its occupants, had been loaded onto a freight train at La Boca for transport to Wright-Patterson Air Base. I was a bit surprised, but agreed it probably was true, when he pointed out to me that La Boca was the closest active freight depot from the reported site of the Aztec saucer crash.

Although transport of a crashed saucer over unroaded, mountainous terrain to get to La Boca would have been difficult, the gentleman was certain that this is where that secret operation was accomplished. To him, the fact that I—who had played a major role in the Air Force-funded Colorado Project, and was therefore obviously involved in the Air Force conspiracy—now appeared as the resident-owner of La Boca, was certain confirmation that La Boca was where the little green men were loaded into railroad cars.

4

An Alien Spacecraft Did Not Crash in Roswell

Robert L. Park

Robert L. Park is a physicist at the University of Maryland in College Park and the director of the American Physical Society in Washington, D.C.

Many UFO enthusiasts believe that an extraterrestrial craft crashed in Roswell, New Mexico, in 1947. On June 14 of that year, William Brazel found a large wreckage on the southwestern ranch where he worked and believed that the debris might have come from a "flying disc." The U.S. Army issued a report saying that the debris was a standard radar target, but Brazel's story about the crashed flying saucer quickly garnered media publicity. For fifty years the myth of the alien spacecraft crash grew more elaborate and exaggerated. In 1997 the government finally issued another report stating that the wreckage was the remains of a large military balloon launched as part of a secret military project (Project Mogul) to detect Soviet atomic bomb tests during the Cold War. There had in fact been a cover-up, but not of an alien spaceship. Nonetheless, some UFO believers are now convinced that because the government lied once, it is still hiding the truth about a UFO in Roswell.

In the summer of 1954, when I was a young Air Force lieutenant, I was sent on temporary assignment to Walker Air Force Base in Roswell, New Mexico, to oversee the installation of a new radar system. Late one night I was returning to the base after a weekend visit with my family in Texas. I was driving on a totally deserted stretch of highway. The sky was moon-

Robert L. Park, "Welcome to Planet Earth," *The Sciences*, May 2000. Copyright © 2000 by the New York Academy of Sciences. Reproduced by permission.

less but very clear, and I could make out a range of ragged hills off to my left, silhouetted against the background of stars. Suddenly the entire countryside was lit up by a dazzling blue-green light, streaking across the sky just above the horizon.

The light flashed on and off as it passed behind the hills, then vanished without a sound. It was all over in perhaps two seconds. At the time, reported sightings of unidentified flying objects—UFOs—made the news almost daily. Indeed, the town where I was stationed, Roswell, was the hub of many such speculations. But I prided myself on being a skeptical thinker, and I had little patience for wacky ideas about flying saucers invading the earth.

In fact, I had a perfectly plausible explanation for the spectacular event I had just witnessed. Pale blue-green is the characteristic color of the light emitted by certain frozen free radicals as they warm up. A free radical is a fragment of a molecule, and one well-known variety of free radical is the so-called hydroxide radical—a water molecule that is missing one of its hydrogen atoms. Free radicals are energetically predisposed to reconnect with their missing parts, and for that reason they are highly reactive: ordinarily they do not stick around very long.

But if molecules are broken up into free radicals by radiation at low temperature, the radicals can be frozen in place. Then, when the severed parts of the molecule are warmed up, they readily recombine to form the same kinds of stable molecules from which they originated. The energy that is liberated when hydroxide radicals recombine with hydrogen atoms to form water appears as blue-green fluorescence. It occurred to me that an ice meteoroid would gradually accumulate hydroxide radicals as a result of cosmic-ray bombardment. What I had had the good fortune to see just then, I reasoned, was a meteor plunging into the earth's upper atmosphere, where it warmed, setting off the recombination reaction.

A "close encounter"

As I continued driving down the empty highway and crossed into New Mexico, I felt rather smug. The UFO hysteria that was sweeping the country, I told myself, was for people who don't understand science. Then I saw the flying saucer.

It was off to my left, between the highway and the distant hills, racing along just above the rangeland. It appeared to be a shiny metal disk, thicker in the center than at the edges, and it was traveling at almost the same speed I was. Was it following me? I stepped hard on the gas pedal of the Oldsmobile—and the saucer accelerated. I slammed on the brakes—and it stopped. Only then could I see that it was my own headlights, reflecting off a telephone line strung parallel to the highway. The apparition no longer looked like a flying saucer at all.

It was a humbling experience. My cerebral cortex might have sneered at stories of flying saucers, but the part of my brain where those stories were stored had been activated by the powerful experience of the icy meteorite. At an unconscious level, my mind was busy making connections and associations. I was primed to see a flying saucer—and my brain filled in the details.

> **" I had little patience for wacky ideas about flying saucers invading the earth. "**

Who has not "seen" an animal in dusky twilight that turns into a bush as one takes a closer look? But something more than the mind playing tricks with patterns of light is needed to explain why hundreds—by some accounts thousands—of people claim to have been abducted by aliens, whisked aboard a spaceship and subjected to some kind of physical examination, usually focusing on their erogenous zones. After the examination, the aliens are frequently said to insert a miniature implant into the abductee's body. Often the memory of an abduction has a dreamlike quality, and subjects can recall the details only under hypnosis. . . .

It is hardly surprising that there are similarities in the accounts of people who claim to have been abducted by aliens. All of us have been exposed to the same images and stories in the popular media. My local bookstore stocks three times as many books about UFOs as it carries about science. Aliens stare at us from the covers of magazines and make cameo appearances in television commercials. As time goes by, the depictions become increasingly uniform. Any six-year-old can now sketch what an alien looks like. Popular culture is, in fact, undergoing a kind of alien evolution: each new creation by a filmmaker or sci-fi writer acts as a mutation, and the selection mechanism is audience approval. Aliens subtly evolve to satisfy public expectations. . . .

The Roswell case

The current fascination with aliens can be traced back to the strange events that took place near Roswell, New Mexico, in the summer of 1947. On June 14 of that year, William Brazel, the foreman of the Foster Ranch, seventy-five miles northwest of Roswell, spotted a large area of wreckage about seven miles from the ranch house. The debris included neoprene strips, tape, metal foil, cardboard and sticks. Brazel didn't bother to examine it closely at the time, but a few weeks later he heard about reports of flying saucers and wondered if what he had seen might be related. He went back with his wife and gathered up some of the pieces. The next day he drove to the little town of Corona, New Mexico, to sell wool, and while he was there he "whispered kind a confidential like" to the Lincoln County sheriff, George Wilcox, that he might have found pieces of one of those "flying discs" people were talking about. The sheriff reported the matter to the nearby army air base—the same base, in fact, where I would be stationed seven years later (before my time, though the Air Corps was still part of the army, and the base was known as Roswell Army Air Field).

> **//** *Various UFO 'investigators' managed to stitch those snippets into a full-scale myth of an encounter with extraterrestrials.* **//**

The army sent an intelligence officer, Major Jesse Marcel, to check out the report. Marcel thought the debris looked like pieces of a weather balloon or a radar reflector; in any event, all of it fit easily into the trunk of his car. There the incident might have ended—except for the garbled account the public-information office at the base issued to the press the next day. The army, the press office noted, had "gained possession of a flying disc through the cooperation of a local rancher and the sheriff's office." The army quickly issued a correction describing the debris as a standard radar target, but it was too late. The Roswell incident had been launched. With the passage of years, the retraction of that original press release would come to look more and more like a cover-up.

By 1978, thirty years after Brazel spotted wreckage on his

ranch, actual alien bodies had begun to show up in accounts of the "crash." Major Marcel's story about loading sticks, cardboard and metal foil into the trunk of his car had mutated into the saga of a major military operation, which allegedly recovered an entire alien spaceship and secretly transported it to Wright Patterson Air Force Base in Ohio. Even as the number of people who might recall the original events dwindled, incredible new details were added by second- and third-hand sources: There was not one crash but two or three. The aliens were small, with large heads and suction cups on their fingers. One alien survived for a time but was kept hidden by the government—and on and on.

A full-scale myth

Like a giant vacuum cleaner, the story had sucked in and mingled together snippets from reports of unrelated plane crashes and high-altitude parachute experiments involving anthropomorphic dummies, even though some of those events took place years later and miles away. And, with years' worth of imaginative energy to drive their basic beliefs, various UFO "investigators" managed to stitch those snippets into a full-scale myth of an encounter with extraterrestrials—an encounter that had been covered up by the government. The truth, according to the believers, was simply too frightening to share with the public.

> *There really had been a cover-up, it turned out—but not of an alien spaceship.*

Roswell became a gold mine. The unverified accounts spawned a string of profitable books, and were shamelessly exploited for their entertainment value on television programs and talk shows—even serious ones, such as CBS's *48 Hours*, then hosted by the eminent anchorman Dan Rather, and CNN's *Larry King Live*. The low point was reached by Fox TV. In 1995 the network began showing grainy black-and-white footage of what was purported to be a government autopsy of one of the aliens—a broadcast that garnered such exceptional ratings (and such exceptional advertising revenues) that it was rerun repeatedly for three years. Then, when ratings finally began to wane,

Fox dramatically "exposed" the entire thing as a hoax.

In 1994, to the astonishment of believers and skeptics alike, a search of military records for information about the Roswell incident uncovered a still-secret government program from the 1940s called Project Mogul. There really had been a cover-up, it turned out—but not of an alien spaceship.

Project Mogul

In the summer of 1947 the U.S.S.R. had not yet detonated its first atomic bomb, but it had become clear by then that it was only a matter of time. It was imperative that the United States know about the event when it happened. A variety of ways to detect that first Soviet nuclear test were being explored. Project Mogul was an attempt to "listen" for the explosion with low-frequency acoustic microphones flown to high altitudes in the upper atmosphere. The idea was not entirely harebrained: the interface between the troposphere and the stratosphere creates an acoustic channel through which sound waves can propagate around the globe. Acoustic sensors, radar tracking reflectors and other equipment were sent aloft on long trains of weather balloons, in the hope that they would be able to pick up the sound of an atomic explosion.

The balloon trains were launched from Alamogordo, New Mexico, about a hundred miles west of Roswell. One of the surviving scientists from Project Mogul, the physicist Charles B. Moore, professor emeritus at the New Mexico Institute of Mining and Technology in Socorro, recalls that Flight 4, launched on June 4, 1947, was tracked to within seventeen miles of the spot where Brazel found wreckage ten days later. Then, Moore says, contact was lost. The debris found on the Foster Ranch closely matched the materials used in the balloon trains. The Air Force now concludes that it was, beyond any reasonable doubt, the crash of Flight 4 that set off the bizarre series of events known as the Roswell incident. Had Project Mogul not been highly secret, unknown even to the military authorities in Roswell, the entire episode would probably have ended in July 1947. . . .

By 1997 the Air Force had collected every scrap of information dealing with the Roswell incident into a massive report, in hopes of bringing the story to an end. . . . Responding to requests from self-appointed UFO investigators acting under the Freedom of Information Act had become a heavy burden on the Air Force staff at the Pentagon, and they were eager to get ahead of the Roswell incident. The release of *The Roswell Report: Case Closed* drew one of the largest crowds on record for a Pentagon press conference.

Although the people involved insist that it was mere coincidence, the Air Force report was completed just in time for the fiftieth anniversary of Brazel's discovery of the Project Mogul wreckage. Thousands of UFO enthusiasts descended on Roswell, now a popular tourist destination, in July 1997 for a golden-anniversary celebration. They bought alien dolls and commemorative T-shirts, and snatched up every book they could find on UFOs and aliens. The only book that sold poorly was the Air Force report.

People still believe in the UFO

If there is any mystery still surrounding the Roswell incident, it is why uncovering Project Mogul in the 1990s failed to put an end to the UFO myth. Several reasons seem plausible, and they are all related to the fact that the truth came out almost half a century too late. The disclosures about Project Mogul were pounced on by UFO believers as proof that everything the government had said before was a lie. What reason was there to think that Project Mogul was not just another one?

> *It is easy to read too much significance into reports of widespread public belief in alien visits to earth.*

Furthermore, Project Mogul was not the only secret government program that bolstered belief in UFOs. During the cold war, U-2 spy planes often flew over the Soviet Union. At first, U-2s were silver-colored, and their shiny skins strongly reflected sunlight, making them highly visible— particularly in the morning and evening, when the surface below was dark. In fact, the CIA estimates that more than half of all the UFO reports from the late 1950s and throughout the 1960s were actually sightings of secret U-2 reconnaissance flights. To allay public concerns at the time, the Air Force concocted far-fetched explanations involving natural phenomena. Keeping secrets, as most people learn early in life, inevitably leads to telling lies.

> **❝** *Secrets and lies leave the government powerless to reassure its citizens in the face of far-fetched conspiracy theories.* **❞**

But secrecy, it seems, is an integral part of military culture, and it has generated a mountain of classified material. No one really knows the size of that mountain, and despite periodic efforts at reform, more classified documents exist today than there were at the height of the cold war. The government estimates that the direct cost of maintaining those records is about $3.4 billion per year, but the true cost—in loss of credibility for the government—is immeasurable. In a desperate attempt to bring the system under control, in 1995 President Bill Clinton issued an executive order that will automatically declassify documents that are more than twenty-five years old—estimated at well in excess of a billion pages—beginning in the year 2000.

The consequence of government secrecy

Recent polls indicate that a growing number of people think the government is covering up information about UFOs. Nevertheless, it is easy to read too much significance into reports of widespread public belief in alien visits to earth. The late astronomer and science popularizer Carl Sagan saw in the myth of the space alien the modern equivalent of the demons that haunted medieval society, and for a susceptible few they are a frightening reality. But for most people, UFOs and aliens merely add a touch of excitement and mystery to uneventful lives. They also provide a handy way for people to thumb their noses at the government.

The real cost of the Roswell incident must be measured in terms of the erosion of public trust. In the interests of security, people in every society must grant their governments a license to keep secrets, and in times of perceived national danger, that license is broadened. It is a perilous bargain. A curtain of official secrecy can conceal waste, corruption and foolishness, and information can be selectively leaked for political advantage. That is a convenient arrangement for government officials, but in the long run, as the Roswell episode teaches, it often backfires. Secrets and lies leave the government powerless to reassure its citizens in the face of far-fetched conspiracy theories. Concealment is the soil in which pseudoscience flourishes.

5

An Extraterrestrial Craft Crashed in Roswell

Philip J. Corso

Philip J. Corso served in the U.S. Army for twenty-one years as an intelligence officer. Since his retirement in 1963, he has worked in both the public and private sector as a security specialist.

In 1947 a flying saucer crashed in Roswell, New Mexico. The U.S. military officially denied that aliens had visited Earth because they did not want to incite mass panic. Top-secret files demonstrate that the army did in fact believe the Roswell craft belonged to extraterrestrials who were a greater threat than the United States' Cold War foes, the Soviet Union and the People's Republic of China. The military studied the advanced technology of the wrecked spaceship and used what they learned to triumph both in the Cold War and in the war against the extraterrestrials.

My name is Philip J. Corso, and for two incredible years back in the 1960s while I was a lieutenant colonel in the army heading up the Foreign Technology desk in Army Research and Development at the Pentagon, I led a double life. In my routine everyday job as a researcher and evaluator of weapons systems for the army, I investigated things like the helicopter armament the French military had developed, the tactical deployment complexities of a theater antimissile missile, or new technologies to preserve and prepare meals for our troops in the field. I read technology reports and met with engineers at army proving grounds about different kinds of ord-

Philip J. Corso with William J. Birnes, *The Day After Roswell*. New York: Pocket Books, 1997. Copyright © 1997 by Rosewood Woods Productions, Inc. All rights reserved. Reproduced by permission of Atria, an imprint of Simon & Schuster Adult Publishing Group.

nance and how ongoing budgeted development projects were moving forward. I submitted their reports to my boss, Lt. Gen. Arthur Trudeau, the director of Army R&D [research and development] and the manager of a three-thousand-plus-man operation with lots of projects at different stages. On the surface, especially to congressmen exercising oversight as to how the taxpayers' money was being spent, all of it was routine stuff.

> ▌▌ *The Roswell file was the legacy of what happened in the hours and days after the crash when the official government cover-up was put into place.* ▌▌

Part of my job responsibility in Army R&D, however, was as an intelligence officer and adviser to General Trudeau who, himself, had headed up Army Intelligence before coming to R&D. This was a job I was trained for and held during World War II and Korea. At the Pentagon I was working in some of the most secret areas of military intelligence, reviewing heavily classified information on behalf of General Trudeau. I had been on General MacArthur's staff in Korea and knew that as late as 1961—even as late, maybe, as today—as Americans back then were sitting down to watch *Dr. Kildare* or *Gunsmoke*, captured American soldiers from World War II and Korea were still living in gulag conditions in prison camps in the Soviet Union and Korea. Some of them were undergoing what amounted to sheer psychological torture. They were the men who never returned.

The government's deepest secrets

As an intelligence officer I also knew the terrible secret that some of our government's most revered institutions had been penetrated by the KGB and that key aspects of American foreign policy were being dictated from inside the Kremlin. I testified to this first at a Senate subcommittee hearing chaired by Senator Everett Dirksen of Illinois in April 1962, and a month later delivered the same information to Attorney General Robert Kennedy. He promised me that he would deliver it to his brother, the President, and I have every reason to believe he did. It was ironic that in 1964, after I retired from the army and had served on Senator Strom Thurmond's staff, I worked for Warren Commission member Senator Richard Russell as an investigator. But hidden beneath everything I did, at the center of a double life I led that no one knew about, and buried deep inside my job at the Pentagon was a single file cabinet that I had inherited because of my intelligence background. That file held the army's deepest and most closely guarded secret: the Roswell files, the cache of debris and information an army retrieval team from the 509th Army Air Field pulled out of the wreckage of a flying disk that had crashed outside the town of Roswell in the New Mexico desert in the early-morning darkness during the first week of July 1947. The Roswell file was the legacy of what happened in the hours and days after the crash when the official government cover-up was put into place. As the military tried to figure out what it was that had crashed, where it had come from, and what its inhabitants' intentions were, a covert group was assembled under the leadership of the director of intelligence, Adm. Roscoe Hillenkoetter, to investigate the nature of the flying disks and collect all information about encounters with these phenomena while, at the same time, publicly and officially discounting the existence of all flying saucers. This operation has been going on, in one form or another, for fifty years amidst complete secrecy.

Why the story was kept quiet

I wasn't in Roswell in 1947, nor had I heard any details about the crash at that time because it was kept so tightly under wraps, even within the military. You can easily understand why, though, if you remember, as I do, the Mercury Theater "War of the Worlds" radio broadcast in 1938 when the entire country panicked at the story of how invaders from Mars landed in Grovers Mill, New Jersey, and began attacking the local populace. The fictionalized eyewitness reports of violence and the inability of our military forces to stop the creatures were graphic. They killed everyone who crossed their path, narrator Orson Welles said into his microphone, as these creatures in their war machines started their march toward New York. The level of terror that Halloween night of the broadcast was so intense and the military so incapable of protecting the local residents that the police were overwhelmed by the phone calls. It was as if the whole country had gone crazy and authority itself had started to unravel.

Now, in Roswell in 1947, the landing of a flying saucer was no fantasy. It was real, the military wasn't able to prevent it, and this time the authorities didn't want a repeat of "War of the Worlds." So you can see the mentality at work behind the desperate need to keep the story quiet. And this is not to mention the military fears at first that the craft might have been an experimental Soviet weapon because it bore a resemblance to some of the German-designed aircraft that had made their appearances near the end of the war, especially the crescent-shaped Horton flying wing. What if the Soviets had developed their own version of this craft?

Varying accounts of Roswell

The stories about the Roswell crash vary from one another in the details. Because I wasn't there, I've had to rely on reports of others, even within the military itself. Through the years, I've heard versions of the Roswell story in which campers, an archeological team, or rancher Mac Brazel found the wreckage. I've read military reports about different crashes in different locations in some proximity to the army air field at Roswell like San Agustin and Corona and even different sites close to the town itself. All of the reports were classified, and I did not copy them or retain them for my own records after I left the army. Sometimes the dates of the crash vary from report to report, July 2 or 3 as opposed to July 4. And I've heard different people argue the dates back and forth, establishing time lines that vary from one another in details, but all agree that something crashed in the desert outside of Roswell and near enough to the army's most sensitive installations at Alamogordo and White Sands that it caused the army to react quickly and with concern as soon as it found out.

In 1961, regardless of the differences in the Roswell story from the many different sources who had described it, the top-secret file of Roswell information came into my possession when I took over the Foreign Technology desk at R&D. My boss, General Trudeau, asked me to use the army's ongoing weapons development and research program as a way to filter the Roswell technology into the mainstream of industrial development through the military defense contracting program. Today, items such as lasers, integrated circuitry, fiber-optics networks, accelerated particle-beam devices, and even the Kevlar material in bulletproof vests are all commonplace. Yet the seeds for the development of all of them were found in the crash of the alien craft at Roswell and turned up in my files fourteen years later.

But that's not even the whole story.

The secret war against aliens

In those confusing hours after the discovery of the crashed Roswell alien craft, the army determined that in the absence of any other information it had to be an extraterrestrial. Worse, the fact that this craft and other flying saucers had been surveilling our defensive installations and even seemed to evidence a technology we'd seen evidenced by the Nazis caused the military to assume these flying saucers had hostile intentions and might have even interfered in human events during the war. We didn't know what the inhabitants of these crafts wanted, but we had to assume from their behavior; especially their interventions in the lives of human beings and the reported cattle mutilations, that they could be potential enemies. That meant that we were facing a far superior power with weapons capable of obliterating us. At the same time we were locked in a Cold War with the Soviets and the mainland Chinese and were faced with the penetration of our own intelligence agencies by the KGB.

> *In those confusing hours after the discovery of the Roswell alien craft, the army determined that in the absence of any other information it had to be an extraterrestrial.*

The military found itself fighting a two-front war, a war against the Communists who were seeking to undermine our institutions while threatening our allies and, as unbelievable as it sounds, a war against extraterrestrials, who posed an even greater threat than the Communist forces. So we used the extraterrestrials' own technology against them, feeding it out to our defense contractors and then adapting it for use in space-related defense systems. It took us until the 1980s, but in the end we were able to deploy enough of the Strategic Defense Initiative, "Star Wars," to achieve the capability of knocking down enemy satellites, killing the electronic guidance systems of incoming enemy warheads, and disabling enemy spacecraft, if we had to, to pose a threat. It was alien technology that we used: lasers, accelerated particle-beam weapons, and aircraft equipped with "Stealth" features. And in the end, we not only outlasted the Soviets and ended the Cold War, but we forced a stalemate with the extraterrestrials, who were not so invulnerable after all.

What happened after Roswell, how we turned the extraterrestrials' technology against them, and how we actually won the Cold War is an incredible story. During the thick of it, I didn't even realize how incredible it was. I just did my job, going to work at the Pentagon day in and day out until we put enough of this alien technology into development that it began to move forward under its own weight through industry and back into the army. The full import of what we did at Army R&D and what General Trudeau did to grow R&D from a disorganized unit under the shadow of the Advanced Research Projects Agency, when he first took command, to the army department that helped create the military guided missile, the antimissile missile, and the guided-missile-launched accelerated particle-beam-firing satellite killer, didn't really hit me until years later when I understood just how we were able to make history.

I always thought of myself as just a little man from a little American town in western Pennsylvania, and I didn't assess the weight of our accomplishments at Army R&D, especially how we harvested the technology coming out of the Roswell crash, until thirty-five years after I left the army when I sat down to write my memoirs for an entirely different book. That was when I reviewed my old journals, remembered some of the memos I'd written to General Trudeau, and understood that the story of what happened in the days after the Roswell crash was perhaps the most significant story of the past fifty years.

6

Alien Abductions Are Real

John E. Mack

Harvard psychiatrist John E. Mack is a well-known researcher of the alien abduction phenomenon. He is the author of Abduction, Nightmares, and Human Conflict, *and* Passport to the Cosmos. *Mack is also founding director of the Program for Extraordinary Experience Research (PEER).*

Alien abduction is, like several other paranormal experiences, an extrarational event in which human beings confront a reality beyond the scientific and material realm. Because it is so difficult to provide rational proof of the abduction experience, people who claim to have been abducted by aliens are often accused of lying or having a mental illness. The problem is that science is limited by its conventional methodology and tools of observation and does not take account of a more mysterious mode of reality. Rather than seeking conventional evidence, investigators must open their minds to the abductees' accounts disclosed through hypnosis. After abduction claims are carefully screened, subjects are put into a state of modified hypnosis in which they answer neutral, nonleading questions about their experiences. The purpose of the hypnosis is not to verify that an abduction has taken place but to explore the emotional intensity of a person's experience.

I have come to regard the alien abduction phenomenon as one among a number of occurrences currently confronting human consciousness, like near-death and out-of-body experiences, strange animal mutilations, the complex crop formations that appear mysteriously in a few seconds in fields of rape and other grains, apparitions of the Virgin Mary, and spontaneous shamanic experiences, which might be described as crossover phenomena (events of various sorts that appear to manifest *in* the material world but seem not to be *of* it). These phenomena seem to violate that barrier, so sacred to the rationalist mind, between the forces of the unseen world and the material realm, giving us "glimpses," in researcher Linda Howe's words, "of other realities."

In a certain sense, any cosmic mystery might at least theoretically be thought of as simply a reflection of laws of the universe or subtler energies that we do not yet comprehend or know how to measure, rather than as "paranormal" or "supernatural." But the alien abduction phenomenon and the other anomalies named above seem to operate so far outside of the laws of physics (as traditionally understood) that they may require a new paradigm of reality to include them as real and an expansion of our ways of knowing to explore them.

Problems with a scientific approach

It seems to me possible that the matters under consideration here will not yield their secrets to the methodologies of science that were evolved to explore phenomena that were accepted as existing entirely within the material world. This is not to say that careful methods of observation and analysis should not be applied to the physical aspects of the alien abduction phenomenon. Yet the investigations of UFO photographs, radar records, missing persons and pregnancies following abductions, reported observations of strange beings, burned earth patches where UFOs presumably landed, bodily lesions and so-called implants removed from experiencers' bodies after abductions, and all the other physical signs associated with the phenomenon, have been relentlessly accompanied by such discrepancies and difficulties in finding certainty or proof that even the most committed explorers have frequently turned against each other with revelations or accusations of insufficient or bogus credentials and cries of hoax, while the doubtful have tended to dismiss the whole matter as hallucination or the paranoid delusion of true believers.

It is as if the agent or intelligence at work here were parodying, mocking, tricking, and deceiving the investigators, providing just enough physical evidence to win over those who are prepared to believe in the phenomenon but not enough to convince the skeptic. In this apparently frustrating situation, there may lie a deeper truth and possibility. It is as if the phenomenon were inviting us to change our ways, to expand our consciousness and ways of learning, to use, in addition to our conventional ways of knowing and observing, methodologies more appropriate to its own complex, subtle, and perhaps ultimately unknowable nature.

An invisible reality

Wallace Black Elk, who, like many native American elders, has had experiences with "disks," "these little people," and telepathic communication with them, mocks the literalness and limited knowing power of scientific materialism. "The scientists call that a UFO," he told [anthropologist William] Lyon, "but that's a joke, see? Because they are not trained; they lost contact with the wisdom, knowledge, power, and gift. So they have to see everything first with their naked eye. They have to catch one first. They have to shoot it down and see what all it is made of, how it was shaped and formed. But their intention is wrong, so *somebody* is misleading those scientists that way. . . . But the biggest joke is on those scientists, because they lost contact with those star-nation people."

> **"** In the case of the alien abduction phenomenon—and perhaps this is true of all 'daimonic realities'—the source is unseen. **"**

We are just beginning to learn how to understand and explore phenomena that might be called intrusions from the unseen or "subtle" realms. What appears to yield the best results, as measured by a steady emergence of information or knowledge, falling short of conventional demands for proof, is a combination of meticulous empirical observation together with carefully recorded narratives of firsthand experiences, matching, sorting, and comparing accounts from many individuals from different locations and cultures. An attitude of not knowing, a kind of Buddhist-like "empty mind," is essential, a willingness to hear and record observations and reports that "do not fit" established schemes or frameworks.

In the case of the alien abduction phenomenon—and perhaps this is true of all "daimonic realities"—the source is unseen. The encounters penetrate into the material world, but these manifestations are elusive, sporadic, and difficult to document convincingly. The greatest source of information is the reports of the experiencers themselves. Here the investigator, if not a mental health professional by training, must become in some sense a clinician, opening himself or herself to information that may threaten intensely any established worldview. Much can be learned just from listening to consciously recollected experience. The use of a nonordinary state of consciousness, however—a relaxation exercise or modified hypnosis—can penetrate more deeply into the mystery of the experiences and help therapeutically to release the powerful emotions held within that seem almost always to be left in the wake of the experiences. . . .

Working with abductees

Since the first publication of *Abduction* [Mack's earlier book] in 1994, I have continued to work intensively with individuals who contact me or PEER [Program for Extraordinary Experience Research] because they suspect that they may have had an abduction encounter. This population is self-selected by virtue of the fact that by now my general orientation toward the abduction phenomenon is fairly well known. First, I do not consider that abduction reports necessarily reflect a literal, physical taking of the human body, nor do I look upon experiencers as victims, although I strive to be empathic in relation to the pain and trauma that they may have undergone. Also, it is known that in my work I have come to regard the phenomenon not merely as a negative and cruel intrusion, which it can be, but also as one that can bring about new understanding of ourselves and our identity in the cosmos.

Psychiatric social worker Roberta Colasanti, who is present during most of the meetings with experiencers, helps to select those with whom we will meet. We can see only a small fraction of those who contact us, but we use no fixed criteria to select them. Generally, we look for people who seem quite clearly to have had anomalous experiences, as suggested by apparent contact during waking hours with an unexplained "presence" (interpreted sometimes as an angel, ghost, spirit guide, or other entity known within the belief structure of a particular culture), or with a nonhuman entity, and/or a close encounter with a UFO, strange unexplained bright lights, periods of missing time, and odd small lesions on the body that seem to have appeared in conjunction with the above indicators.

The screening process

Individuals contact us primarily by letter or phone. Roberta, as the clinical director of PEER, screens individuals with the use of a structured telephone interview. The intention of this screening tool is to help rule out gross mental illness, substance abuse, and suicidality. If the individuals need psychiatric help, Roberta will refer them to an appropriate therapist or clinical facility. Once the individual has been appropriately screened, he or she is asked to write a brief letter specifying the reason for contacting us and providing basic biological information. The individual is offered an initial appointment, so that we may determine the benefit from the contact and gain knowledge that will further our understanding. There are occasions when we decide, after meeting with an individual, that the person is not an experiencer or that even if he or she is experiencing anomalous events, it is not in the individual's best interest to pursue further investigations at that time. In 1996 we received funding to work with cases where there was more than one witness to a particular abduction experience, so we are currently guided by this requirement.

The initial interview usually takes at least two hours, for we must establish trust, take a full personal history, examine the individual for possible psychiatric symptoms that may or may not relate to the presenting reason for coming, and of course review in detail the story of the possible abduction encounters or other anomalous experiences. Sometimes a relative or other individual is present, who may serve as a support person or corroborating witness. Because of the importance, in the multiple-witness project, of keeping reports uncontaminated, we usually interview relatives and other possible witnesses separately.

The effectiveness of hypnosis

A modified hypnosis or relaxation exercise may be used to help focus the client's attention upon their inner experience and memories, but it should be emphasized that about 80 percent of the information is obtained through conscious recollection. In this slightly altered state of mind, it is easier for the individual to recall more fully their experiences, which are usually not deeply repressed, and to begin to discharge the intense energies that seem to be held as if in the very tissues of the body. We are careful not to lead individuals or to encourage them to "produce" an abduction story—we use neutral, encouraging comments and questions. But we must enter deeply into the experiencer's world in order to create trust and to help them tell their story and "hold" the power of the experiences as they relive them. Sometimes the recall appears to be so emotionally intense that it seems as if each experience is being relived in the present moment.

> // We are careful not to lead individuals or to encourage them to 'produce' an abduction story— we use neutral, encouraging comments and questions. //

Psychiatrist C. Brooks Brenneis has framed well the dilemma clinicians face in doing any sort of exploration that seeks to recover memories. "Leaning in the direction of doubt," he writes, "threatens betrayal," while "leaning in the direction of belief" promotes fabrication. "If one does not believe, no memory can be tolerated; and if one does believe, whatever memory appears is suspect." Our clients will return to us as often as seems to be needed to integrate their experiences emotionally, and also for help living in a society that does not even recognize, at least among its elite, the vast realms of being to which they have been opened. Needless to say, this integration is never altogether satisfactory.

Challenges for researchers

What I have written so far might apply *fundamentally* to any sort of psychological study or exploration of emotionally powerful experiences. But working with abduction experiencers requires something different from working with any other patients, clients, or research populations. This is difficult to express clearly, but it has to do with the capacity to let go more fully of one's ego boundaries in order to follow the experiencers into whatever energy field or nonordinary state of consciousness they may take us to as they remember or relive an encounter. At the same time, we must provide a holding container for the intense emotions and energies that come forth (experiencers may sweat, sob, shake, or scream during these sessions), while retaining an observing, mindful presence that maintains appropriate control of the process. Psychologist Shelley Tanenbaum comes close to describing this process when she writes of "an intuitive way of knowing based on the body as experienced during moment-to-moment self-observation or mindfulness"

After we had been working together for more than two years, Will [an abductee participating in the research program] was asked to write a brief article for PEER's newsletter about his understanding of our way of learning together. He wrote of "another way" of knowing that is "not rational, not irrational" but is based on "direct perception." This is a different "frequency setting," an inner or intuitive way, "another voice" to which we often do not listen. This voice, Will writes, is itself a state of remembering that has always been within us, but to discover or rediscover it, our minds must choose "to open this window."

Trust and truthfulness

And there are other challenges. For what we hear may seem so bizarre or impossible from the standpoint of the worldview in which we were brought up that our minds rebel and want to intervene with the reality-testing confrontations that psychiatrists know so well. But to do this would abort communication and destroy trust. We are, of course, aided in this curious "suspension of disbelief" by the fact that we are concerned only with the authenticity and honesty of the client's report, and the presence or absence of psychopathology or another biographical experience that might account for it. There is no injunction to establish the literal or material actuality of the reported experiences.

Our conviction of the truthfulness of what is being witnessed comes from the sheer intensity of feeling and its appropriateness to what is being reported; the consistency of the narrative with work with other clients; the absence of apparent secondary gain or other motive; and finally a judgment, which may be quite subtle and not always correct, that the individual is being as truthful as he or she is able to be. Surely, as the poet Rainer Maria Rilke wrote, we must be prepared "for the most strange, the most singular and most inexplicable that we may encounter."

7

John Mack's Alien Abduction Theory Is Not Credible

James Gleick

James Gleick is an author, journalist, and essayist who has written extensively about science and technology. His books include Chaos: Making a New Science *and* Genius: The Life and Science of Richard Feynman.

John Mack and his alien abduction theory have received a great deal of media coverage, despite the outrageousness of his claim that 4 million Americans have been kidnapped by extraterrestrials. Mack's status as a Harvard psychiatrist and Pulitzer Prize winner lends him some credibility that other alien abduction believers lack. Yet Mack's research methodology is weak and flawed, and his ideas are more influenced by popular culture and Eastern mysticism than by science. Mack is abusing his position as a psychiatrist by leading people to believe they have been abducted by aliens.

In the world of professional wrestling, fans fall into two categories, known as the Smarts and the Marks. The Marks believe that they are watching spontaneous contests of strength and skill. The Smarts know that they are watching a fascinating, highly plotted, roughly scripted form of dramatic entertainment—a sort of sweaty soap opera. The Smarts and the Marks have a lot to talk about, though their conversation sometimes seems at cross-purposes. They have both developed

James Gleick, "The Doctor's Plot," *The New Republic*, May 24, 1994. Copyright an enthusiastic appreciation for the phenomenon, but on different levels.

In the world of unidentified flying objects, John E. Mack (or, as his book jacket labels him. "John E. Mack, M.D., the Pulitzer Prize-winning Harvard psychiatrist") is a Mark masquerading as a Smart.

Mack believes that little gray aliens have been abducting Americans in large numbers and subjecting them to various forms of unwilling sex. (Yes, that again.) Mack also believes that, for a bunch of cosmic rapists, these aliens are a pretty benign bunch. They're trying to bring us in touch with our spiritual sides, or trying to remind us how important it is to care about the planet, or otherwise trying to help our consciousness evolve.

But you already know this—unless you've missed him . . . on [TV show] *Oprah* in the *New York Times* Magazine, on [TV show] *48 Hours*, and in supermarket tabloids, talk shows, and news programs across the country.

> **❝** Mack believes that little gray aliens have been abducting Americans in large numbers and subjecting them to various forms of unwilling sex. **❞**

Alien abduction mythology has been one of this country's tawdry belief manias since the 1960's. It is a leading case of the antirational, antiscience cults that are flourishing with dismaying vigor in the United States, and with dismayingly little counterbalance from people who ought to know better—the Smarts. UFO's in general, paranormals who bend spoons, parapsychologists who sense spiritual auras, crystal healers, believers in reincarnation, psychic crime-solvers—all of these natural descendants of Tarot-readers and crystal-ball-gazers get uncritical television time and newsprint. It's a dangerous trend. The blurring of distinctions between real knowledge and phony knowledge leaves all of us more vulnerable to faith healers and Holocaust-deniers of all sorts.

The new wave of marketing the abduction myth has been grotesquely effective. The *New York Times Book Review* chose to give Mack's new book, *Abduction: Human Encounters with Aliens*, a major illustrated review written by another psychiatrist who has spent time interviewing supposed abductees. This reviewer, James S. Gordon, criticizes some of Mack's methods, but hails him for giving "visibility to a phenomenon that is ordinarily derided" and concludes that Mack "has performed a valuable and brave service, enlarging the domain and generosity of the psychiatric enterprise."

An abduction epidemic is implausible

Let's stop right here and consider, hypothetically, for the first and last time in this article, the possibility that Americans really are being kidnapped by aliens in vast numbers.

All right. We're undergoing a large-scale invasion by gangs of alien sex abusers. There are millions of victims, according to Mack and his fellow abduction proponents. To begin with, is this a matter that should be handled by psychiatrists? Wouldn't astronomers and physicists have some interest in the matter as well? Shouldn't these kidnappings be reported to law-enforcement authorities (they virtually never are)? Wouldn't they be of interest to the FBI, the military, and, say, world leaders?

> *Shouldn't these kidnappings be reported to law-enforcement authorities (they virtually never are)? Wouldn't they be of interest to the FBI, the military, and, say, world leaders?*

The publishers, Charles Scribner's Sons, promote the book with a dust jacket claiming that these are "alien encounters reported in no previous book on UFOs," that they are "real experiences," that Mack's book is "above all authoritative." Do they believe this, individually? According to their hype, one in fifty of their own friends and relatives have been abducted by these little gray rapists—are they, in real life, worrying about this? Similarly, do the editors of the *Times Book Review,* or the television news directors who are helping promote this book with equal foolishness, seriously believe these claims? No, they do not. All these people are Smarts, at heart. Their news departments aren't wasting any time investigating this story, though surely a galactic sex crime of this magnitude would be worth assigning at least as many reporters as the question of whether the President's wife [Hillary Rodham Clinton] once made a killing in commodities.

"Statistics show that 4 million Americans have been abducted . . ." began a Fox TV news item about the Mack book the other day. (It continued with unidentified footage of realistic-looking aliens, from a science-fiction movie. There are no standards left, it seems, in the world of television news.)

> **❝** *What really makes Mack different from the standard flying-saucer nut is that he's got authority.* **❞**

We'll all be hearing this statistic incessantly . . . so it's worth showing once and for all where it comes from. It is the product of a 1991 study conducted by the Roper Organization under the sponsorship of abduction buffs, who mailed their interpretation of the results—titled *Unusual Personal Experiences: An Analysis of the Data from Three National Surveys*—to tens of thousands of mental-health professionals.

The Roper pollers read a list of experiences to 6,000 people and asked them whether they had undergone these experiences, as a child or an adult, more than twice, once or twice, or never (a construction that routinely generates more positive responses than the straightforward ever or never).

The relevant experiences were:

- *Waking up paralyzed with a sense of a strange person or presence or something else in the room.*
- *Experiencing a period of time of an hour or more, in which you were apparently lost, but you could not remember why, or where you had been.*
- *Seeing unusual lights or balls of light in a room without knowing what was causing them, or where they came from.*
- *Finding puzzling scars on your body and neither you nor anyone else remembering how you received them or where you got them.*
- *Feeling that you were actually flying through the air although you didn't know why or how.*

Most healthy people can answer yes to a few of these. I certainly can. They are all well known feelings and dream types. Even the sinister-sounding scar question is an easy yes for many people (take a moment to examine your body carefully and you'll see what I mean).

Flawed assumptions

The answers to these five questions form the entire basis for the alien-abduction statistic. Are you wondering how a respectable survey organization could take these and produce a claim that "one out of every fifty adult Americans may have had UFO abduction experiences"? Easy. The authors had only to make a single fraudulent assumption:

"Based upon the data we have collected, we decided to regard only [!] those respondents who answered 'yes' to at least four of our five key indicator questions as probable abductees."

That was 119 people. Hence—simple arithmetic from here on—4 million Americans.

Perhaps Mack is embarrassed enough by the absurdity of this exercise not to rely on it heavily. He mentions it only once in his book. But he did put his Harvard Medical School imprimatur on the original report, writing the introduction and enclosing a helpful mail-in card for his readers.

> *These aliens, clumsy as they are about anaesthesia and scars, have a way of making the experience vanish from the conscious minds of all 4 million of their American victims.*

The alien-abduction phenomenon began in 1966 with the case of Betty and Barney Hill. They were a New Hampshire couple who—years after having got lost one night in the White Mountains—read some UFO literature, spent a fair amount of time with psychiatrists, finally underwent hypnosis and "remembered" having been kidnapped by aliens and subjected to various indignities. Scores of books, movies, and television docudramas followed as the genre evolved—Barney Hill himself was portrayed by James Earl Jones. For the entertainment industry, this isn't a cultural nuisance; it's a cash cow. And every few years some author finds a new way to cash in, as Whitley Strieber did with his 1987 fiction-posing-as-nonfiction best-seller *Communion*.

Mack has a new angle. "None of this work," he writes, "in my view, has come to terms with the profound implications of the abduction phenomenon for the expansion of human consciousness, the opening of perception to realities beyond the manifest physical world and the necessity of changing our place in the cosmic order if the earth's living systems are to survive the human onslaught."

Mack's manipulation of his authority

What really makes Mack different from the standard flying-saucer nut is that he's got authority.

"Ordinarily," Oprah declared. "we would not even put people on television, on our show certainly, who make such bizarre claims. . . . But we were intrigued by this man. . . . Dr. Mack is a respected professor who teaches at Harvard University. He is an eminent psychiatrist. . . ." The promotion surrounding his new book, *Abduction*, leans heavily on his professional trappings. There is his status as a medical doctor and psychiatrist. There is his Pulitzer Prize (won not for anything to do with UFO's, of course, but for a biography of T. E. Lawrence published 17 years ago). There is Harvard University, where Mack enjoys the comfort of academic tenure.

Mack's publicists—besides Scribner's, he uses a New Jersey firm, PR with a Purpose Inc—are combining and recombining these elements in sleazy ways. A press release begins: "Abduction by aliens was not a topic taken seriously at Harvard University, until John E. Mack, a medical doctor and professor of psychiatry . . ." (Of course it is still not a topic "taken seriously" at Harvard, except to the extent that Mack and fellow gulls happen to be on campus.)

> *As for his own biases, Mack claims he began as a skeptic, but this he is clearly not.*

For readers, *Abduction* will seem a cross between the Whitley Strieber genre and the Nancy Friday sort of one-sexual-fantasy-after-another-as-told-to-me genre. Ed has sex in a "pod" with a silvery-blond alien and finds it "fulfilling" and "great." Catherine is forced to lie on a table naked and spread her legs while an alien with cold hands inserts an instrument into her vagina. Eva is fondled by three "midgets." And so on. It's all excruciatingly unpleasant and incoherent. Just about everyone gets painful needles in the brain or the leg, and just about everyone gets a lecture about pollution or global consciousness on the way out.

The core of Mack's belief is the following cocktail-party syllogism:

> People think they were abducted. They don't seem crazy. (And we ought to know—we're experts on mental illness.)
>
> *Therefore* people were abducted.

It sounds more respectable in psychiatrist talk, naturally: "Efforts to establish a pattern of psychopathology other than disturbances associated with a traumatic event have been unsuccessful. Psychological testing of abductees has not revealed evidence of mental or emotional disturbance that could account for their reported experiences." Ergo . . .

No one remembers their abductions right away. These aliens, clumsy as they are about anaesthesia and scars, have a way of making the experience vanish from the conscious minds of all 4 million of their American victims. (Why is abduction such a peculiarly American phenomenon, by the way? Our national borders aren't visible through the portholes of those spaceships. Mack has an answer: abductions are global, but it's only in the United States that we are lucky enough to have large numbers of UFO-obsessed therapists to help people uncover their suppressed experiences.) Abduction psychiatrists like Mack need a method of helping people remember, and that method is hypnosis.

You are getting sleepy . . . when you awake you will remember. . . . Hypnosis is all about suggestion. It has always been a fringe practice, as useful to carnival magicians and movie-makers as to clinical psychiatrists, and for every genuine buried memory unearthed by a hypnotist, many more false memories have been implanted. At its best, the process is a conspiracy between hypnotist and willing subject. *Time* magazine has quoted one of Mack's subjects as saying that she was given UFO literature to read in preparation for her sessions and was asked obvious leading questions. [Cartoonist] Garry Trudeau has shined his own form of common sense on the process in a *Doonesbury* sequence that has a hypnotized subject saying "Now I see a . . . a blinding light."

"It's a vehicle, isn't it? Some sort of space vehicle?" the hypnotist prompts.

"I . . . I can't tell, It has Nevada plates."

Shaky methodology

From a scientific point of view, Mack's anecdotes are grossly lacking in respectable methodology. He doesn't provide information about his hypnotic techniques, though he does give the impression that there's a lot of breathing involved. He provides no data from psychological tests. These are "time-consuming and expensive," he notes—gosh, right, in that case, why bother? There is nothing remotely resembling a control or a negative case. There is no explanation of how he selected *Abduction's* 13 case studies from his total caseload of 76, except for the following: ". . . there are abductees I have known longer or worked with in greater depth. If I have chosen not to tell their stories here it is because I could not do justice to the richness of their experiences in a sufficiently clear and concise manner." (In other words, there's even better stuff in his files—he just couldn't squeeze them into these 422 pages.)

> *What does John Mack really believe (assuming that the whole thing isn't just a calculated scam)?*

It's never clear where Mack finds his subjects or who they are. They seem to be shuttled to him by the UFO/abduction network, and particularly by Budd Hopkins, author of two 1980's best-sellers on the phenomenon. It was Hopkins who introduced Mack in 1990 to his first four supposed victims and then began a regular series of referrals. Mack's anecdotal descriptions give only a cardboard sense of who they are—despite the torturous physical detail, there is little to flesh out his sweeping claim that "they seem to come, as if at random, from all parts of society." It seems safe to say that there's one kind of patient that Mack never sees: a person suffering from vague and unexplained feelings of anxiety or trauma who, without any familiarity with UFO books or movies and without any suggestion whatsoever on the part of psychiatrist or hypnotist, then remembers an abduction experience. If he had any of those, it would be interesting to see the transcripts. In reality, though, by the time Mack sees them, his patients know very well what they're in for and have been well prepped.

A 1960s late-bloomer

As for his own biases, Mack claims he began as a skeptic, but this he is clearly not. He's a firm believer, for example, in auras— "the energy fields around us that some especially sensitive people can see" He is certainly (much like his aliens) one of the many people who began talking a lot over the past decade or two about saving the planet, protecting the environment, understanding spirituality, and so forth. Mack seems to have been a sixties late-bloomer, falling belatedly and hard for Werner Erhard, Carlos Casteneda, est, Esalen, and so forth. It's really no wonder his abductees find themselves getting such a warm dose of mind expansion along with the extraterrestrial sex abuse.

Mack never manages to discuss the world's most widely shown piece of popular entertainment on his subject, *Close Encounters of the Third Kind*, though surely many, if not all, of his patients saw Steven Spielberg's lovable little bug-eyed aliens long before they came up with their own memories of virtually identical aliens. In fact Mack's whole new mood about abductions isn't new at all—it's all there in *Close Encounters:* the Eastern mysticism, the spiritual save-the-planet denouement. (Remember the closing sound-track of the original version? *"When you wish upon a star,/Makes no difference who you are./Anything your heart desires will come . . . to . . . you."*

The entire issue of contaminating influences is constantly being swept under Mack's rug. He writes at one point, "Eva had written in her journal that she had started to read Whitley Strieber's *Communion*, but discontinued it so as not to be 'influenced by anyone or anything.'" Oh, sure. Anyway, all this scientific, methodological criticism rolls off believers like water off a duck. It's merely "rational" or "empirical" or, worst of all, "Western" (generic terms of dismissal). Mack knows his hypnotism sessions are a collaboration, and he's unrepentant:

"I cannot avoid the fact that a co-creative process such as this may yield information that is in some sense the product of the intermingling or flowing together of the consciousnesses of the two (or more) people in the room," he says. "Something may be brought forth that was not there before in exactly the same form. Stated differently, the information gained in the sessions is not simply a remembered 'item,' lifted out of the experiencer's consciousness like a stone from a kidney. It may represent instead a developed or evolved perception, enriched by the connection that the experiencer and the investigator have made.

"From a Western perspective this might be called 'distortion'; from a transpersonal point of view the experiencer and I may be participating in an evolution of consciousness."

Mack's position is illogical

Arguing with someone who uses language in this blousy manner is like dancing with smoke. It is useless to find errors in reasoning or logic. Logic? What an beggarly, earthbound affair. There are moments when you find yourself wondering whether even Mack knows what he's claiming. With all his harrowing descriptions of rapes and torture, he's still capable of retreating to, ". . . we do not know what an abduction really is— the extent, for example, to which it represents an event in the physical world or to which it is an unusual subjective experience with physical manifestations." This sounds almost sane. I would translate it into my boring kind of English as "we don't know whether abductions are real events or fantasies." And *physical manifestations* is a nice little addendum—it glides right past the fact that there are no physical manifestations, if this means tangible evidence the aliens might have left behind. They're wonderfully tidy about their needles and handcuffs.

> **//** *Sadly, in the age of depth psychology and transpersonal psychology, hypnotherapy and psychic healing, willing professional dupes are in ready supply.* **//**

Mack continues: "A still greater problem resides in the fact that memory in relation to abduction experiences behaves rather strangely." Why, yes! ". . . the memory of an abduction may be outside of consciousness"—translation: *nonexistent*— "until triggered"—translation: *created*—"many years later by another experience or situation that becomes associated with the original event." Such as, maybe, going to the drive-in and watching, [the film] *Close Encounters?* Mack continues (and by the way, does Harvard offer its professors any course in remedial English?): "The experiencer in a situation such as this could be counted on the negative side of the ledger *before* the triggering experience and on the positive side *after* it." In plain language: it's hard to count the people who have been abducted, because if someone says he hasn't been abducted, he may just not remember—yet.

Sigh.

Though he is in all the machinery surrounding his book as true a believer as can be, still, in the actual text, he engages in a slippery form of rhetoric—as if somehow he still wanted to hedge his bets. He writes of "the actual experience (whatever the source of these experience may ultimately prove to be)." What does John Mack really believe (assuming that the whole thing isn't just a calculated scam)? Does he have any curiosity about the technology of this species, on the one hand capable of passing through walls and beaming people about on rays of light, and on the other hand, sometimes reduced to flagging down cars? Does he believe that creatures from another planet are grabbing our fellow humans, pinning them down, and engaging in weird sex with them? Literally?

Mack is evasive

Well, yes—and no. Certainly he writes as though he does, but he also manages to avoid answering such tacky direct questions. Sometimes he switches over to writing in terms of "the abduction phenomenon" (Smartspeak) instead of "abductions" (Markspeak). Mack says, "Our use of familiar words like 'happening,' 'occurred,' and 'real' will themselves have to be thought of differently, less literally perhaps"—it's a sickeningly corrupt style of hiding behind language. His writing is full of phrases drained of all meaning: "the collapse of space/time"; "the alien being opened Ed's consciousness." And there is always the ultimate hedge: "the problem of defining in what reality the abductions occur."

We know some realities they aren't occurring in. They aren't occurring in the reality Mack calls "the ontological framework of modern science." This is the reality where we might be tripped up by things like "accepted laws of physics and principles of biology." They aren't occurring in "the Judeo-Christian tradition"—Jews and Christians have become such stick-in-the-muds compared to (no surprise here) "Eastern religions, such as Tibetan Buddhism, which have always recognized a vast range of spirit entities in the cosmos . . ." Things that, after all, could not have really happened, are constantly happening in "converging time frames" or "another dimension." The game of let's-find-another-reality turns someone like me into such a party-pooper, having to fall back on the common-sense idea that reality is in fact . . . reality.

But it's not just a game. Mack is a practicing psychiatrist, and he's toying with real people. There is "Ed," who first got in touch with Mack in 1992 and "recalled" having been abducted, raped (not Mack's word), and lectured to about "the way humans are conducting themselves here in terms of international politics, our environment, our violence to each other, our food, and all that"—all this having supposedly occurred 31 years earlier, in 1961, though Ed didn't begin to recall it until 1989.

In a chilling aside, Mack writes that Ed and his wife, "Lynn," have had "a number of fertility problems, which may or may not be abduction-related, including three or four spontaneous terminations of Lynn's pregnancies." It's a reminder: This man is practicing medicine. He is telling patients that their miscarriages may be due to imaginary aliens. Why do the medical licensing boards permit this?

"Abductees" target the mental health profession

Mack represents the most visible agent of an especially disturbing trend in the UFO landscape: mailings and publicity targeted specifically at psychologists and psychiatrists. Private organizations financed by abduction devotees are spending money to persuade these professionals that there is something clinically respectable about looking for UFO's along with, say, child abuse in their patients' troubled histories. Mack's own tax-exempt funding source is his Center for Psychology and Social Change. He also has a Program for Extraordinary Experience Research. These organizations want clinicians to look for abduction cases whenever they encounter such tell-tale symptoms as (I'm quoting from a 1992 Mack mailing to mental-health professionals) "fears of the dark and of nightfall."

Sadly, in the age of depth psychology and transpersonal psychology, hypnotherapy and psychic healing, willing professional dupes are in ready supply. It seems that anything goes these days in the mental-health business. Even more sadly, psychiatrists are exactly the people who should be treating the scores of people who think they have been abducted by aliens and who should be trying to understand the phenomenon.

For there *is* an abduction phenomenon, and it's worth studying. Cultural historians might think fruitfully about the shared details of the abduction mythology, at least to the extent that they can be disentangled from the influences of the self-referential movies and books that victims have been exposed to. [Scientist] Carl Sagan has pointed out similarities with old (pre-space-age) stories of incubi and succubi, witches and fairies.

> *Scores or perhaps even hundreds of people do 'remember' having been kidnapped by aliens, and this needs to be understood. There is an explanation.*

"Is it possible," he wrote [in 1993], "that people in all times and places occasionally experience vivid, realistic hallucinations, often with sexual content—with the details filled in by the prevailing cultural idioms, sucked out of the *Zeitgeist*. When everyone knows that gods regularly come down to Earth, we hallucinate gods; when everyone knows about demons, it's incubi and succubi; when fairies are widely believed, we see fairies; when the old myths fade and we begin thinking that alien beings are plausible, then that's where our hypnagogic imagery tends."

The limits of rationality

The problem is that, by and large, the Smarts aren't interested in arguing with the Marks. It seems unprofitable, when no amount of rational discourse can change the mind of a believer. A few worthy organizations devote themselves to this sort of thing, most notably the *Committee for the Scientific Investigation of Claims of the Paranormal*, publishers of the *Skeptical Inquirer*. But most astronomers, physicists, and paleontologists have better things to do, though they are the sorts of people best equipped to explain just how infinitely unlikely it is that our corner of the universe should be receiving alien visitors in such strikingly near-human form at just the eyeblink of history when we have discovered space travel. Outside of hard science, all too many academics have fallen into the literary conceit that anyone's version of reality is as valid as anyone else's, and here in the real world, it's a conceit with bad consequences.

Not that mental-health workers have nothing to contribute to understanding phenomena like the abduction myth. On the contrary—scores or perhaps even hundreds of people do "remember" having been kidnapped by aliens, and this needs to be understood. There is an explanation. As with so many belief manias, the explanation is unwelcome to many people:

We are not fully rational creatures.

Our minds are not computers. We see people, we hear voices, we sense presences that are not really there. If you have never seen the face of someone you know, in broad daylight, clear as truth, when in reality that person was a continent away or years dead, then you are unusual.

Our memories cannot be trusted—not our five-minute-old memories, and certainly not our decades-old memories. They are weakened, distorted, rearranged, and sometimes created from wishes or dreams. With or without hypnosis, we are susceptible to suggestion.

The painful irony is that of all the people—the Smarts— who should know these lessons and articulate them for the rest of us, none are better placed than professors of psychiatry.

8

People Are Drawn to the Spiritual Aspects of UFOs

Irving Hexham and Karla Poewe

Irving Hexham is a professor of religious studies at the University of Calgary, where his wife, Karla Poewe, is a professor of anthropology. They are the coauthors of New Religions as Global Cultures: Making the Human Sacred.

The controversy over UFOs is usually characterized as a dispute between rationalists and "true believers" in the paranormal. But belief in extraterrestrial beings also has a strong spiritual dimension. Writers in the nineteenth and early twentieth century cast their ideas about extraterrestrial life in often explicit spiritual terms. In the 1960s and 1970s, several important books identified space aliens as godlike beings and their appearance on earth as a sign of the coming apocalypse. UFO cults espouse notions of creation, providence, and salvation that are similar to those found in many traditional religious doctrines.

Years ago British anthropologist E.E. Evans-Pritchard went to live among the Azande people in Africa. An educated person of the West and a social scientist, Evans-Pritchard rejected the witchcraft beliefs of the Azande. But he began to recognize that to live and work among the Azande one had to assume the reality of witchcraft. Once this was done, social practices fell into place and the world made sense. He found that to live in an Azande village required a leap of the imagination without which it was impossible to obtain the basic necessities of life. Only by acknowledging the reality of witchcraft could he negotiate the basic transactions needed to keep him alive.

Attempting to understand the logic that led 39 well-educated people [in 1997] to commit suicide because they believed they would be transported to a higher level of being by way of a spacecraft that was tailing the Hale-Bopp comet requires a similar leap of the imagination. Usually we associate UFOs with science, possible other worlds and hard-nosed science fiction. Most discussions of UFOs concern 1) the question of whether there is scientific evidence for them and 2) theories about extraterrestrial life. All this seems a far cry from the pseudo-theosophical and gnostic ideas propagated on the Heaven's Gate[1] Higher Source Web site.

Spirituality and extraterrestrials

But at least since the time of the first "flying saucer" craze of the early 1950s, interest in UFOs has been closely tied to matters of spirituality.

The suggestion that extraterrestrials regularly visit the earth was first made by the American journalist Charles Fort (1874–1932). In *The Book of the Damned* (1919) and other books, Fort argued that modern science represented a new kind of "priescraft," which, he claimed, refused to admit certain inconvenient truths. Presenting a monistic vision of the universe, Fort systematically replaced Christian ideas of creation and providence with a form of secular spirituality involving godlike extraterrestrials.

Many early science fiction writers, including Damon Knight (1922-), Eric Frank Russell (1905–1978) and Sam Moskowitz (1920-), were influenced by Fort. More important, his ideas about extraterrestrials observing and guiding human development were adapted by E.E. "Doc" Smith (1890–1965) in *Triplanetary* (1934), which he developed into his "Lensmen" series in 1948. This highly popular series united numerous spiritual ideas and mythological themes into a hi-tech space opera. George Lucas's Star Wars movies were consciously modeled on the Lensmen books.

Another writer influenced by Fort was Richard Shaver

---

1. Heaven's Gate was the cult that led thirty-nine of its members to commit suicide in 1997.

(1907–1975), who created a sensation in March 1945 when his story "I Remember Lemuria" appeared in *Amazing Stories*. This fantastic yarn about lost civilizations generated an intense controversy. A series of sequels followed, leading to the publication of the books *I Remember Lemuria* and *The Return of Santhanas* in 1948.

The first UFO books appeared in 1950. Most of these were uninteresting descriptions of strange lights in the sky. In 1953 Desmond Leslie and George Adamski published *Flying Saucers Have Landed*. Adamski claimed to be the first human to have encountered space aliens visiting earth in UFOs. Significantly, both Adamski and Leslie, like Fort and Shaver before them, engaged in theosophical speculation. Long before they used science fiction to transform theosophical concepts into pseudoscientific claims about UFOs, these writers were deeply immersed in occult literature. From the beginning, UFO stories were entangled with religious beliefs of theosophical origin supported by rich occult mythologies.

> **❝** *From the beginning, UFO stories were entangled with religious beliefs of theosophical origin supported by rich occult mythologies.* **❞**

Following the success of Leslie and Adamski, a host of other spiritually inclined writers made similar claims. The most important of these was Erich von Däniken, whose book *Chariots of the Gods?* (1968) purported to be a serious study of strange evidence suggesting that spacemen once visited the earth. Shaver's influence on von Daniken is clear. Later, in *The Gold of the Gods* (1972), von Daniken dropped his pseudoscientific stance to reveal his true religious interests. Other books, like Brad Steiger's *Gods of Aquarius* (1976) and Jacques Vallee's *Messengers of Deception* (1979), continue to blur the distinction between science and religion, empirical reality and the occult.

Surveys show that between 70 and 75 percent of North Americans believe in extraterrestrials and UFOs. Consider also the much smaller, but growing, number of people who claim contact with UFOs and/or abduction by space aliens, and the plot thickens.

The best-known religion that has developed out of a fascination with UFOs is L. Ron Hubbard's Scientology. Hubbard's first works were science-fiction adventure stories. In 1938 he published "The Dangerous Dimension" in the magazine *Astounding*, and he eventually became one of the magazine's most prolific writers.

In 1950 he published *Dianetics*, which he proclaimed as a "new science of the mind." In the background of this science was Hubbard's fascination with interplanetary travel. One of the earliest and most enthusiastic converts to Dianetics was none other than *Astounding's* charismatic editor John W. Campbell, who did all he could to promote Hubbard's views through his magazine. Other science fiction writers such as Katherine MacLean, James Blish and Kurt van Vogt were drawn into the enthusiasm, although later all moved away from Hubbard's movement.

Various other new religions were founded by people who had dabbled in Scientology, the most successful being EST and Eckankar. The most infamous is the Heaven's Gate community, whose leaders studied Scientology in the early 1970s.

The spread of UFO cults

Meanwhile, other UFO cults emerged. These included the Wallace Halsey's Christ Brotherhood; the Association of Sananda and Sanat Kumara made famous in *When Prophecy Fails* (1955), written by Leon Festinger, Henry W. Riecken and Stanley Schachter; and George King's Aetherius Society, founded in 1955. Today the Unarius movement, which expects salvation in 2001, and the Realians, who say that 2035 is a more likely date, are the most influential of these movements. More recently, UFO beliefs have gained ground among fundamentalist Christians through the writings of men like Texe Marrs and Gary North. They give UFOs a demonic spin, regarding them as part of a cosmic conspiracy threatening Christianity.

Behind all these movements and beliefs lies a mythology of creation which rejects evolution as a scientific concept but which, except in the case of the fundamentalists, cannot accept a biblical view of creation. UFOs are regarded as the vehicles of creation, providence and final salvation. This spiritualized universe resembles early gnosticism in its emphasis on escaping from earthly existence into lost worlds and other civilizations that provide a higher (nonmaterial) realm of existence. Modern gnostics would object to applying the term to Heaven's Gate, but the religious themes are indeed strikingly similar.

9

Scientists Are Taking UFOs Seriously

Rick Del Vecchio

Rick Del Vecchio is a staff writer for the San Francisco Chronicle.

Pilots' reports of firsthand encounters with UFOs are inspiring scientists to seriously investigate the mysterious phenomena. While most UFO reports have glaring credibility weaknesses, at least several dozen documented incidents cannot be easily dismissed. Scientists are beginning to consider all possible explanations, from secret military technology to extraterrestrial crafts to a lack of knowledge about physical reality. The government's fear of inciting mass panic is insufficient reason for quashing investigations of UFO sightings, especially those reported by military and civilian pilots.

It was a routine flight from San Francisco to Boston. The DC-10 was on autopilot, with World War II combat veteran Neil Daniels in the captain's seat.

Suddenly, the jumbo jet veered to the left. Daniels looked out the window and saw something odd over the winter cloud tops.

He didn't recognize it, and 25 years later, the Los Altos [California] resident still can't figure out what it was.

"There was this brilliant, brilliant light, the intensity of a flashbulb," Daniels said.

It was round, like a quarter held at arm's length. As ground control asked for a report on the unplanned swerve, Daniels'

Rick Del Vecchio, "Fighting the Fear Factor: Local Scientists Are Quietly Working to Give UFO Sightings a Measured Look and Lend Legitimacy to Those Who Spot Them," *San Francisco Chronicle*, January 12, 2003. Copyright © 2003 by the *San Francisco Chronicle*. Reproduced by permission of Copyright Clearance Center, Inc.

first officer took the controls. The plane resumed course and the floater shot away at a slight upward angle.

"It upset the compasses on the airplane, so it was a magnetic force of some intensity," Daniels said.

It was, by any other name, a UFO.

Pilot sightings of UFOs

Few pilots in those days dared say they saw one. That unidentified flying objects were unmentionable was all but national policy. The attitude came out of America's Cold War fears and deep-down pragmatism: If it's not square, it must be kooky.

Daniels' boss discouraged him from reporting the bogie. The two other members of the flight crew clammed up.

Daniels had survived 29 bombing missions over Germany and would log 30,000 hours in his flying career. He'd seen a lot, but nothing like this. He soon found he wasn't alone.

> **//** *Something with the reflexes of a bird of prey double-swiped a French Mirage fighter at right angles over Dijon in 1977. During the encounter, the pilot felt he was being 'watched.'* **//**

Other pilots tipped him that they, too, had crossed paths with a UFO. There were so many stories like his that Daniels wondered who was hiding what—and why. "There's been an enormous coverup," he said.

Now the retired pilot is playing a small role in a national effort to end America's UFO-phobia.

The story of his 1977 encounter south of Syracuse, N.Y., has made its way into the case files of a sober-sided research panel called the National Aviation Reporting Center on Anomalous Phenomena.

Headed by former NASA scientist Richard Haines of Los Altos, the year-old group is one of several private organizations saying that UFOs deserve a measured, scientific look. With research helpers around the country, it's a confidential sounding board for professionals in the taboo-bound aviation field.

Haines' focus is on helping flight and ground crews safely handle something many have experienced but few have talked about. "Everybody's so God-darned afraid of everything," Daniels said.

Challenges to science

Wingless, noiseless, metallic-looking or luminous curiosities have been reported to interact with aircraft since Daniels flew B-17s over Germany. In their 60-year modern career, they've paced planes in level flight and in turns and dives, hovering, zigzagging, bouncing, pulsing, zooming and otherwise upending the rules of flying. Haines has clocked the average length of plane-oddity contact at nearly six minutes.

> *Some researchers say what's needed is not only good evidence but also a different way to look at reality.*

"How does science rationally deal with a phenomenon that stays with an airliner at high altitude (and) at high speed for 20 minutes?" he asked. "It automatically eliminates a long list of mundane phenomena."

Haines' group has collected 1,300 pilot reports and is gathering more from government and private sources in many countries. "This is kind of snowballing," said Ted Roe of Vallejo, the group's executive director. "First off, we're learning that the phenomenon is distributed globally."

Witnesses, often quite shaken up, note the unknowns' outlandish speed and agility in solo and formation flight. Something with the reflexes of a bird of prey double-swiped a French Mirage fighter at right angles over Dijon in 1977. During the encounter, the pilot felt he was being "watched."

Observers also are impressed by UFOs' geometric shapes, which are unlike any known airfoil. And their lighting schemes make no aviation sense: blinding whites, glowing greens and oranges, multicolored flashers like haywire Christmas trees.

"During the day, they are solid, three-dimensional surfaces that reflect sunlight," Haines said. "Eighty percent of the night-time sightings are self-luminous. My personal belief is they are the same set of phenomena."

They act as if they're looking for something, but—don't

communicate. They intimidate, but only in the movies do they annihilate. "When shot at," Haines said, "the phenomenon doesn't shoot back."

They are so furtive as to appear self-disguising behind all manner of plasmoid morphings, vanishings and high-speed acrobatics.

It would appear they don't want any trouble. But for science, they've been nothing but.

A cautious approach

It's all a magic show of the mind, most scientists tend to think. Few have ventured in. But Haines is attracted because he believes a conservative approach can gain on the mystery.

A former NASA behavioral scientist who worked on manned moon missions and later helped design aircraft cockpit displays, he has published more than 70 journal articles in his specialty. He prides himself on his caution.

Haines is interested in mundane meteorological, geological and astronomical origins, apart from the more far-out possibilities popularly associated with UFOs. Opinion polls show that almost half the American public believes they're from outer space.

Haines and allied researchers are investigating the elusive and possibly electrical "blue sprites" pilots see in the upper atmosphere, the links between floating lights and sacred sites and whether incoming meteors can be seen on radar.

> *//'It's that Roswell crap again,' is what the ground controller told a nearby Air Force base after the pilot of a commercial flight spotted a UFO over New Mexico in March 1995.//*

Haines stands apart from the UFO culture and even from the acronym itself. He instead likes UAP, for unidentified aerial phenomenon. The coinage is picking up currency: Scientists and aviation experts adopted the acronym for a November conference at George Washington University in Washington, D.C., on aerial mysteries and interstellar travel.

"(Haines') approach is an end-run," said Minneapolis documentary filmmaker Tom Tulien, whose Project Sign gathers oral histories of pilots and military servicemen who have encountered UFOs.

"It defuses the issue as most people understand it," he said. "We're not interested in proving UFOs are real—we're interested in the implications of the phenomenon."

The scientific debate

Haines is among the elves in a worldwide circle of aerial mystery puzzlers that stretches as far away as public research groups in Chile, Norway and Turkey, and as close as America's zipper-mouthed government and science establishments. Part of what keeps the effort going is its silent partnership with insiders who want to help science without hurting their good names.

"Science is so close-minded that they're unwilling to look at the evidence," said Haines, relaxed in retirement in his *Sunset* magazine-neat Peninsula ranch house.

Some have the same complaint about UFO believers, who tend to focus more on theories than on evidence.

"The battle lines are drawn," said UFO historian Jan Aldrich of Canterbury, Conn., whose Project 1947 is archiving the UFO story in America. "It's E.T., or it's stupid."

Despite strange marks and burns on the ground, radiation traces, skyfalls of magnesium, tin and tungsten carbide, and a handful of genuine photos of unknown metallic-looking flying objects, physical proof of UFOs as non-human handiwork doesn't exit. This is a given, except to those who hold that the government has the story and is sitting on it.

But stripping out more than 99.9 percent of the reported cases still leaves a richly bizarre one every few years. Studies in other fields have gone on less. With UFOs, researchers say, there is more.

"The fact of the matter is, there does exist a vast amount of high quality, albeit enigmatic, data," Redwood City astronomer Bernard Haisch states in introducing himself to visitors to a Web site he has created, Ufoskeptic.org. He is also one of Haines' top associates in the aerial mystery group.

Much of the data rests on witness reports, and that presents a problem: The senses are easily fooled. The stranger the sensation, the harder the brain tries to make sense of it.

But there are at least a few dozen records with enough witness credibility and narrative detail to impress Haines and his league that some fraction of the UFO mystery is physically real. A 1999 French think-tank study put the number of "remarkable, that is to say, credible, well-documented cases" worldwide in recent decades in the hundreds.

"Underneath it all, the truth is there," Roe said, "but you have to be very discriminating."

A multifaceted approach is needed

UFOs aren't just a problem for hard science. The mystery, it seems, is too complicated for it to be understood from any one angle to see it whole.

"I'd be willing to entertain the possibility that the UFO phenomenon is real and may be a manifestation of something more profound than visits from another planet," Haisch said.

Society should take a long look from many sides without being in a hurry for answers—"in the same way astronomical observations were made for centuries without being able to make sense of things," he said.

One of today's more patient sky watchers is scientist Erling P. Strand. He works with Norway's Project Hessdalen, which observes strange, varied lights that glide about the Hessdalen Valley.

He said there are so many shapes and varieties that it's hard to believe only one source is involved: species of round, oval, bullet-shaped and cylindrical lights, some lasting microseconds, others staying for hours.

"The cylinders are sometimes horizontal, sometimes vertical," Strand said. "These cigar-shaped lights do not always have light all over the surface. Sometimes they are described as with a black area in the middle.

"This black phenomena has mostly a yellow light in both ends," he said, "but they can also be seen with two yellow lights in one end and a red in front. The shape then is more triangular."

There are blue lights, too. "And sometimes," Strand said, "there are several different colors at the same time."

Some researchers say what's needed is not only good evidence but also a different way to look at reality. Space isn't empty, it's made of energy. Mass, motion, gravity—all side effects. What seems solid, isn't. Then it would be the universe that's strange, not any form that fizzles in and out of the narrow band of human perception. . . .

UFO sightings and flight crews

Haines doesn't have to know the answers to know that the phenomenon affects people in a real way.

He wants to see international aviation reporting standards, because he says encounters not only upset crews but also instruments and could, in rare cases, cause accidents. The 1999 French study offered similar advice.

Haines has found 57 cases, including Daniels', where aircraft instruments were affected during an encounter. Pilots have experienced spinning compasses and dead radios in addition to intense light and heat in the cockpit.

"The authorities could acknowledge that they don't know everything," he said. "The second thing is, let's at least be open-minded enough about it to encourage pilots to report what they are seeing. They're not even doing that."

Case in point: the 757 and the flying cigar.

"It's that Roswell crap again," is what the ground controller told a nearby Air Force base after the pilot of a commercial flight spotted a UFO over New Mexico in March 1995.

Silhouetted by lightning against distant clouds, it was a spindle at least 300 feet long. It had strobing lights in an unfamiliar pattern.

> *It's commonly believed not only that UFOs are vehicles from space but also that their secrets have been known to establishment information-controllers for decades.*

The operator called the military's air-defense network: "It's right out of 'The X-Files [TV show].' I mean, it's definitely a UFO or something like that. . . ."

Told of the object's size, the air-defense spotter said, "Holy smokes!" And the flashing cigar sailed off into the night, the watchers none the wiser.

The sighting took place over an area known for its secret military reservations and Native American mysticism. It's also a historic UFO hotspot, with two reputed crashes and a landing on the books.

For Roe, the cigar remains on record as a classic UFO in its appearance and in the human response it provoked: an unknown solid, wingless object that transfixed a half-dozen people, all trained professionals.

"You watch that mouse freeze when it looks at a hawk—it's that same vibe," he said. "I have a lot of empathy for humans who are dealing with this."

Roe, in a written analysis of the event, did not lay blame but concluded that the stigma surrounding the subject created a barrier to communication.

"It is remarkable," he wrote. Roe concluded "that a radar/visual observation of a flying object lacking a transponder code and larger than any known fixed-wing aircraft, twice the length of a 747 and hurtling through controlled U.S. air space at 390 knots, would be managed so casually."

Modern UFO "outbreaks"

The modern UFO era began in 1943 with pilot sightings of aircraft-pacing lights over Europe during World War II. It broke open in 1947 with the first civilian reports of "flying saucers."

The last major outbreak was in the early 1970s, but enough activity still goes on to keep private reporting organizations busy. The National UFO Reporting Center [NUFORC] lists more than 50 cases from Northern California in the last year, which go on top of a worldwide stack of tens of thousands since 1947.

In May 2001, a music teacher in Fair Oaks, outside Sacramento, and three students were driving home from an outing when they saw something metallic and triangular over a tree, according to an unverified NUFORC report. It took off in a frightful manner.

"One of the kids started to cry and become hysterical, yelling out, 'Go, go!'" the teacher reported. "I turned my eyes and hit the throttle. All three cried out, almost shrieking, because the craft had shot straight up in the sky and disappeared."

Long before aliens, abductions and Area 51,[1] there were airships and "aeronauts." In pre-aviation 1896 and 1897, sightings of one or more Jules Verne-like flying vehicles made news from coast to coast. They played brilliant white lights over Sacramento on Nov. 18, 1896, and over Oakland five days later.

1. top-secret military base in Nevada that many believe to be a site of government experiments with UFO technology

Some said they whizzed around at an amazing 60 mph.

UFO apparitions have changed over the ages. In biblical and medieval times, people wrote of aerial dragons, shields, swords and crosses. In Victorian days, they saw mechanical contraptions. Fifty years ago, the skies were full of saucers. In the present age of stealth, the archetypal form is, like the latest high-tech military planes, triangular.

But one thing about the mystery hasn't changed: the tendency to belittle witnesses. . . .

Secrets and conspiracies

It's commonly believed not only that UFOs are vehicles from space but also that their secrets have been known to establishment information-controllers for decades. The gatekeepers have locked away the truth, motivated by a desire to keep the power structure intact or by a twisted patriotism: The public couldn't handle the shock.

Congress must investigate, say groups such as the Disclosure Project and the Extraterrestrial Political Action Committee, both based in Maryland but with followings in California. They are taking up a cause championed in the 1960s by a University of Arizona astronomer who challenged the establishment.

It's possible Earth is being watched by aliens, a University of Arizona at Tucson scholar, James E. McDonald, told a congressional subcommittee in 1968. He also charged that "the scientific community has been seriously misinformed for 20 years."

That same year, the government-sanctioned Condon Report found only a relative handful of UFO encounters to be unexplained and none of the 701 worth more bother. Case closed, said the skeptics.

McDonald, who had looked into 300 cases on his own, lost his fight to change the system from the inside. But his disciples would partially vindicate him.

They got declassified records showing that the government maintained a low-key watch on UFOs long after officially closing the book. They said the authorities had good reason to be keenly interested, if there was anything to the reports of such witnesses as Robert Salas.

Salas, a former Air Force captain, told of strange predawn events on March 17, 1967, in his underground nuclear missile post at Montana's Malmstrom Air Force Base.

A topside guard, "practically screaming," phoned Salas with

strange news: a glowing red object was hovering over the main gate.

Salas called the command post. "As I was talking, the missiles starting shutting down," the Los Angeles resident said in an interview.

Salas, sworn to secrecy and knowing the ICBMs were designed so that a serial crash was all but impossible, could only speculate. "The thing wanted to shut us down to show that it could," said Salas, a prime witness in the Disclosure Project's push for congressional hearings.

Salas' opinion is controversial. His credibility isn't.

"Bob Salas is solid as solid can be," filmmaker Tulien said.

> **❝** *In 1973, a National Guard pilot plunged his helicopter over Ohio to avoid a streaking object he felt was 'coming to take us out.'* **❞**

Salas said he is prepared to round up multiple witnesses to back him up. He "defies anybody" to shoot down his story. But he hasn't been invited to put his account on the official record, and most people think the politics of UFOs probably won't allow that to happen.

The government's official silence could mean only that the authorities are as much in the dark as anyone, though few Americans believe this. It could mean they don't know enough to end the debate. But one thing is clear: the rare U.S. and British official inquiries over the years haven't solved a thing.

More mysterious sightings

What Graham Bethune saw was flying. It was a saucer.

And it was headed straight for him.

In 1951, he was a Navy flier on a mission off Newfoundland when he saw a yellowish light hovering over the North Atlantic. It looked like the glow of a city. Then it rose.

In a spilt second it closed 15 miles to become a 300-foot-wide oval on a crash course with his patrol plane.

"It made this run at us," said Bethune, 80, who lives in Toms River, N.J.

Bethune plunged the plane as the oval went over his wing.

Compass needles spun. The crew hit the deck.

"The navigator busted his head," he said. "There was quite a lot of excitement, I can tell you that."

Then the oval suddenly braked and reversed like a rebounding ball.

UFOs and military aircraft

UFOs have performed some of their most striking displays around military aircraft.

In 1973, a National Guard pilot plunged his helicopter over Ohio to avoid a streaking object he felt was "coming to take us out." It stopped dead in front of the chopper, a gray metallic submarine shape with a dome and weird, bright lights, reminding a crewman of something out of a cartoon.

In Belgium in 1990, a flying triangle accelerated from 174 to 1,118 mph and dropped nearly a mile in altitude when pursuing F-16s made radar contact with it. The time of the maneuver was one second.

A brilliantly lit cylinder north of Tehran discharged a smaller object at a pursuing fighter in 1976. The pilot tried to shoot but the weapons controls of his American-made F-4 went dead, a detail that concerned the U.S. military. The pilot banked to get away. The object tagged along on the inside of his turn. Then it broke off and rejoined the cylinder.

> *The CIA guy says, 'OK, you're all sworn to secrecy. This event never happened, we were never here, and we're confiscating all the data.'*

The Tehran tube was so bright that the pilot had to delay his landing because he was temporarily blinded. It also strobed all colors at a phenomenal rate.

Photos of such close encounters are rare. But in 1988, the pilot of a private plane pacing a glider over Palm Springs chanced to click his shutter the moment a fast-moving metallic sphere sliced through the sky beyond the sailplane. Haines has studied the image in detail.

The pilot described the object as a "shiny ball bearing." In the photo, it's concealed in mist. The image shows a white contrail behind a round but indistinct head. The trail doesn't reflect sunlight as a stream of water vapor would. The head sports tiny tendrils of white light at right angles to the direction of travel. Both details are odd, but conclusive of nothing.

"It does not appear to be a lifting body, like an airplane," Haines said. "The reason being, it was a sphere. I had to do some research on the aerodynamics of spheres. But the problem with spheres is there's as much lift on the top as there is on the bottom, so the net effect is gravity.

"This did not come down," he said, "It continued to fly out of sight with a straight contrail."

Haines estimated the chrome globe's speed at from 857 to 4,000 mph. No one reported hearing a sonic boom.

Haines has taken his investigation as far as he can. "I don't know if science could take it any further," he said.

CIA pressure

Kenju Terauchi was sure he had met up with an advanced technology high in the sky.

Piloting a Japan Air Lines 747 cargo flight near Fairbanks in November 1986, he saw two unknown objects the size of smaller airliners but with structural details, lights and maneuvers he didn't recognize.

In the middle distance of a clear night, he also saw the outline of a ringed orb he described as the size of two aircraft carriers. The sight worried him.

Radar in the plane and on the ground saw something in the area of the strange outline, which paced the 747 at a fixed distance.

Terauchi circled. The object stayed in formation. After another airliner pulled up to take a look, Terauchi signaled with his landing lights and saw the object blink out.

The FAA [Federal Aviation Agency] announced that the radar blips were shadows from the 747. But the explanation was inconsistent with the data, said John Callahan, the FAA accident investigator who led the analysis of the radar records.

Callahan, now retired, recalled that the blips indicated the presence of an unknown object that was too fast for radar to get a steady fix on it. "It was something moving 2,000 to 3,000 miles an hour, or faster," he said.

He said the military radar records in the case were recycled before FAA investigators could review them, and the CIA took over the investigation.

"The CIA guy says, 'OK, you're all sworn to secrecy. This event never happened, we were never here, and we're confiscating all the data,'" Callahan said.

He said he asked the agent what he thought the pilot saw.

"'It's a UFO. We can't tell the American public we're being visited by UFOs. It would scare the hell of out 'em.'"

Organizations to Contact

The editors have compiled the following list of organizations concerned with the issues debated in this book. The descriptions are derived from materials provided by the organizations. All have publications or information available for interested readers. The list was compiled on the date of publication of the present volume; the information provided here may change. Be aware that many organizations take several weeks or longer to respond to inquiries, so allow as much time as possible.

Center for the Study of Extraterrestrial Intelligence (CSETI)
PO Box 265, Crozet, VA 22932-0265
(301) 249-3915 • fax: (501) 325-8328
e-mail: coordinator@cseti.org • Web site: www.cseti.org

CSETI is a nonprofit research and educational organization that is dedicated to establishing peaceful and sustainable contact with extraterrestrial life-forms. Its goal is to establish contact with and educate society about extraterrestrial intelligence. The center publishes numerous position papers and field reports on UFOs.

Citizens Against UFO Secrecy, Inc. (CAUS)
PO Box 20351, Sedona, AZ 86341-0351
(602) 818-8248
Web site: www.caus.org

CAUS is a nonprofit public interest group that believes that extraterrestrial intelligence is in contact with earth and that there is a campaign of secrecy to conceal this knowledge. Its goals are to educate and enlighten the public about this cover-up and to fund further research into extraterrestrial contact with earth.

Committee for the Scientific Investigation of Claims of the Paranormal (CSICOP)
PO Box 703, Amherst, NY 14226
(716) 636-1425 • fax: (716) 636-1733
e-mail: info@csicop.org • Web site: www.csicop.org

Established in 1976, the committee is a nonprofit scientific and educational organization that encourages the critical investigation of paranormal and fringe-science claims from a scientific point of view. It disseminates factual information about the results of such inquiries to the scientific community and the public. CSICOP publishes *Skeptical Inquirer* magazine, the children's book *Bringing UFOs Down to Earth*, and bibliographies of other published materials that examine claims of the paranormal.

Federal Bureau of Investigation (FBI)
Headquarters, J. Edgar Hoover Building
935 Pennsylvania Ave. NW, Washington, DC 20535-0001
(202) 324-3000
Web site: www.fbi.gov

The FBI hosts an official Web site that includes, among other things, an electronic reading room. The reading room offers all published FBI findings and articles on UFOs, with such topics as "Animal/Cattle Mutilation," and "Roswell."

J. Allen Hynek Center for UFO Studies (CUFOS)
2457 W. Peterson Ave., Chicago, IL 60659
(773) 271-3611
e-mail: infocenter@cufos.org • Web site: www.cufos.org

CUFOS is a nonprofit scientific organization dedicated to the continuing examination and analysis of the UFO phenomenon. The center acts as a clearinghouse for the reporting and researching of UFO experiences. It publishes the quarterly *International UFO Reporter*, the *Journal of UFO Studies*, monographs, and special reports.

Mutual UFO Network, Inc. (MUFON)
PO Box 369, Morrison, CO 80465-0369
(303) 932-7709
e-mail: HQ@mufon.com • Web site: www.mufon.com

The Mutual UFO Network, Inc., is an international nonprofit scientific organization founded in 1969 that studies, researches, and investigates UFOs by drawing on the grassroots efforts and fields of expertise of its members. MUFON maintains a Web site, publishes a monthly journal, and holds annual symposia.

National UFO Reporting Center
PO Box 45623, University Station, Seattle, WA 98145
(206) 722-3000
Web site: www.ufocenter.com

Founded in 1974, the center serves as a headquarters for reporting possible UFO sightings. Such reports are recorded and disseminated for objective research and information purposes. The center maintains an on-line database of all reports and also publishes a monthly newsletter.

SETI League
PO Box 555, Little Ferry, NJ 07643
(201) 641-1770 • fax: (201) 641-1771
e-mail: info@setileague.org • Web site: www.setileague.org

The SETI League is a membership-supported, nonprofit educational and scientific organization dedicated to the search for extraterrestrial intelligence. Its publications include the books *Project Cyclops* and the *SETI League Technical Manual* as well as the quarterly newsletter *SearchLites*.

Skeptics Society
PO Box 338, Altadena, CA 91001
(818) 794-3119 • fax: (818) 794-1301
e-mail: skepticmag@aol.com • Web site: www.skeptic.com

The society is composed of scholars, scientists, and historians who promote the use of scientific methods to scrutinize such nonscientific beliefs as religion, superstition, mysticism, and New Age beliefs. It is devoted to the investigation of extraordinary claims and revolutionary ideas and to the promotion of science and critical thinking. The society publishes the quarterly *Skeptic Magazine.*

Society for Scientific Exploration (SSE)
PO Box 3818, Charlottesville, VA 22903
fax: (804) 924-4905
Web site: scientificexploration.org

Affiliated with the University of Virginia's Department of Astronomy, the society seeks to provide a professional forum for presentations, criticisms, and debates concerning topics that are ignored or given inadequate study by mainstream academia. It strives to increase understanding of the factors that at present limit the scope of scientific inquiry. The society publishes the quarterlies *Journal of Scientific Exploration* and *Explorer.*

Ufomind
PO Box 81166, Las Vegas, NV 89103
(702) 227-1818 • fax: (702) 227-1816
Web site: www.ufomind.com

Ufomind hosts the world's most extensive Web site on UFOs and paranormal phenomena, and it seeks to provide a forum where all sides can be heard on these issues. The Web site houses a research index and a bookstore.

Bibliography

Books

Robert E. Bartholomew and George S. Howard — *UFOs and Alien Contact; Two Centuries of Mystery.* New York: Prometheus, 1998.

C.D.B. Bryan — *Close Encounters of the Fourth Kind.* New York: Alfred A. Knopf, 1995.

Albert Budden — *Electric UFOs: Fireballs, Electromagnets, and Abnormal States.* New York: Sterling, 1998.

Philip J. Corso with William J. Birnes — *The Day After Roswell.* New York: Pocket Books, 1997.

Phil Cousineau — *UFOs: A Manual for the Millennium.* New York: HarperCollins West, 1995.

Roy Craig — *UFOs: An Insider's View of the Quest for Evidence.* Denton: University of North Texas Press, 1995.

Paul Devereux and Peter Brookesmith — *UFOs and Ufology: The First 50 Years.* New York: Facts On File, 1997.

Richard M. Dolan and Jacques F. Vallee — *UFOs and the National Security State: Chronology of a Coverup, 1941–1973,* revised ed. Hampton Roads, VA: Hampton Roads, 2002.

Bill Fawcett — *Making Contact: A Serious Handbook for Locating and Communicating with Extraterrestrials.* New York: Morrow, 1997.

Steven M. Greer — *Extraterrestrial Contact: The Evidence and Implications.* Afton, VA: Crossing Point, 1999.

Michael Hesemann and Philip Mantle — *Beyond Roswell: The Alien Autopsy Film, Area 51, and the US Government Coverup of UFOs.* London: Michael O'Mara, 1997.

Budd Hopkins — *Witnessed: The True Story of the Brooklyn Bridge UFO Abductions.* New York: Pocket Books, 1996.

David M. Jacobs — *The Threat: Revealing the Secret Alien Agenda.* New York: Simon and Schuster, 1995.

Philip J. Klass — *The Real Roswell Crashed-Saucer Coverup.* Amherst, NY: Prometheus, 1997.

Kal K. Korff — *The Roswell UFO Crash: What They Don't Want You to Know.* Amherst, NY: Prometheus, 1997.

James McAndrew — *The Roswell Report: Case Closed.* Washington, DC: U.S. Government Printing Office, 1997.

Barry Parker   *Alien Life: The Search for Extraterrestrials and Beyond.* New York: Plenum, 1998.

Phil Patton   *Dreamland: Inside the Secret World of Roswell and Area 51.* New York: Random House/Villard, 1998.

Curtis Peebles   *Watch the Skies! A Chronicle of the Flying Saucer Myth.* Washington, DC: Smithsonian Institution Press, 1994.

Kevin J. Randle   *Project Blue Book Exposed.* New York: Marlowe, 1997.

Robert Sheaffer   *UFO Sightings: The Evidence.* Amherst, NY: Prometheus, 1998.

Whitley Strieber   *Confirmation: The Hard Evidence of Aliens Among Us?* New York: St. Martin's, 1999.

Periodicals

Robert E. Bartholomew   "Before Roswell: The Meaning Behind the Crashed-UFO Myth," *Skeptical Inquirer,* May/June 1998.

Susan Blackmore   "Abduction by Aliens or Sleep Paralysis?" *Skeptical Inquirer,* May/June 1998.

Thomas Carroll   "Dreamland," *Fate,* April 1996.

Hugh F. Cochrane   "High Strangeness from Within," *Fate,* July 1998.

Roger Downey   "People Who Run with Aliens," *Seattle Weekly,* September 30–October 6, 1999.

Bernard D. Gildenberg and David E. Thomas   "Case Closed: Reflections on the 1997 Air Force Roswell Report," *Skeptical Inquirer,* May/June 1998.

Becky Harris   "UFOs: Looking for Little Green Men in Shag Harbour," *Maclean's,* December 30, 2002.

Leon Jaroff   "Did Aliens Really Land?" *Time,* June 23, 1997.

Leslie Kean   "UFO Theorists Gain Support Abroad, but Repression at Home," *Boston Globe,* May 21, 2000.

Art Levine   "A Little Less Balance, Please," *U.S. News & World Report,* July 14, 1997.

Gerry Loughran   "After Half a Century, It's RIP for the UFOs," *Africa News Service,* May 17, 2002.

Michael P. Lucas   "Venturing from Shadows into Light," *Los Angeles Times,* September 4, 2001.

Jill Neimark   "The Harvard Professor & the UFOs," *Psychology Today,* March/April 1994.

Omni   "The Roswell Declaration," October 1994.

Theodore Roszak   "The Moral Truth Is Out There," *San Jose Mercury News,* July 6, 1997.

Randall Rothenberg	"Area 51, Where Are You? Route 375 in Nevada Declared 'Extraterrestrial Highway,'" *Esquire*, September 1996.
Robert Sheaffer	"The Truth Is, They Never Were Saucers," *Skeptical Inquirer*, September/October 1997.
Robert Sheaffer	"UFOs Hot and Cold," *Skeptical Inquirer*, September/October 2003.
Glenn G. Sparks, Marianne Pellechia, and Chris Irvine	"Does Television News About UFOs Affect Viewers' UFO Beliefs? An Experimental Investigation," *Communication Quarterly*, vol. 46, Summer 1998.
Dennis Stacy	"Cosmic Conspiracy: Six Decades of Government UFO Cover-Ups, Part I," *Omni*, April 1994.
John Starr	"The Sighting," *Sky & Telescope*, May 1996.
Jacques Vallee	"Consciousness, Culture, and UFOs," *Noetic Sciences Review*, Winter 1995.
Michael Warren	"A Rift in the UFO Ranks," *Final Frontier*, November/December 1996.
Jim Wilson	"Roswell Plus 50," *Popular Mechanics*, July 1997.
Jim Wilson	"The Secret CIA UFO Files," *Popular Mechanics*, November 1997.

Index